Eros, Eros, Eros

SELECTED AND LAST POEMS

Eros, Eros, Eros

Selected and Last Poems

BY ODYSSEAS ELYTIS

Translated from the Greek by Olga Broumas

COPPER CANYON PRESS
Port Townsend, Washington

Printed in the United States of America.

Grateful acknowledgment is made to the following publications, in which some of the poems from this book first appeared: *The Agni Review, The American Poetry Review, The American Voice, The Great River Review, The Poughkeepsie Review, Willow Springs, Zyzzyva.*

The Greek publishers of the original texts are Ikaros Books and Ypsilon Books.

The publication of this book was supported by grants from the Lannan Foundation, the National Endowment for the Arts, and the Washington State Arts Commission, and by contributions from Elliott Bay Book Company, James Laughlin, and the members of the Friends of Copper Canyon Press. Copper Canyon Press is in residence with Centrum at Fort Worden State Park.

LIBRARY OF CONGRESS CATALOGING-IN-PUBLICATION DATA

Elytis, Odysseas, 1911–1996
[Poems. English. Selections]
Eros, eros, eros : selected and last poems / by Odysseas Elytis;
translated from the Greek by Olga Broumas.
   p. cm.
ISBN 1-55659-083-0
1. Title.
PA5610.E43 A22 1998
889'.132 — DDC21   98-19741
               CIP

COPPER CANYON PRESS
Post Office Box 271
Port Townsend, Washington 98368

Contents

for Ioulíta Heliopoulou

A Paradise of One's Own: Odysseas Elytis

Odysseas Elytis is a poet like no other in this world. Neither the lead-
ing figure in a literary movement nor a famous teacher of younger
poets, he follows a line of individualistic visionary ecstatic poets leading
all the way back to Sappho in the sixth century BCE.

He credits his art primarily to two moments of supreme insight.
The first came one night in 1929 when the eighteen-year-old Elytis
chanced upon a book by Paul Éluard, a moment reified in 1935 when
Elytis, then a student at the School of Law, University of Athens,
attended a lecture on surrealism by Andréas Embirícos. He left the
university without his degree, and began a long friendship with Em-
birícos and association with other new Greek poets such as George
Seferis and Nikos Gatsos. With publication of *Orientations* in 1939
and *Sun the First* in 1943, Elytis established himself as one of the great
lyric voices of modern poetry.

What had attracted the young Elytis to surrealism was not its
revolutionary rejection of traditional versification nor its stream-of-
consciousness, but its faith in intuition and passionate exploration of
the subconscious imagination. Imagination is as much "reality" as the
temporal physical world around us. Surrealism was a means by which
to return to the original source, a poetics that would reject the con-
ventions of rational discourse in traditional verse, admitting dream,
reverie, and dissociative imagery. The early poems shimmer with
transparent light. Kimon Friar, in his brilliant introduction to *The
Sovereign Sun: Selected Poems* (Temple University Press, 1974), called
them a "Dionysian exaltation not heard since the outpourings of Sike-
lianós, or the erotic optimism of Embirícos. Elytis showed himself
in finer control of his technique, more translucent in his images,
clearer in his expression. In *Orientations* and *Sun the First*, he became
the foremost lyric poet of his generation; in him the deification of

youth amid the legendary landscape and sweet reveries of the Aegean Sea received its apotheosis."

The second great revelation came after Mussolini invaded Greece in October, 1940, and the fall of Elytis's homeland, Crete, in 1941, beginning more than three years of Axis occupation. Elytis, a lieutenant in the First Army Corps, says in an interview with Ivar Ivask, "It became necessary for me to proceed toward that spear-point where life and death, light and darkness cease to be contraries.... Fear, the physical fear of war, the material fear of bombs and shells, annihilated within me all aspects of false literature and left naked the meaning of a true need for poetry. Fear was in turn annihilated in me by the salvation brought me, as a man, by a poetry made of nakedness and truth."

In the harsh Greek landscape, splendid as it may be, youth passes quickly, and the eighteen-year-old sun-dazzled boy-god was to convey the countenance of middle age by thirty. In 1943, Elytis composed *Heroic and Elegiac Song for the Lost Second Lieutenant of the Albanian Campaign*, a symphonic *tour de force* drawing on the powers of traditional demotic poetry, surrealist elements introduced with even greater restraint as the poet began to find a voice that would speak for an entire nation. His lyric was not of liquid sunlight on Aegean shores, but of how "agony stoops with bony hands." Years later, he would write in a letter to Kimon Friar, "I believe in the restitution of justice, which I identify with light. And together with a glorious and ancient ancestor of mine, that 'I do not care for those gods whose worship is practiced in the dark.'"

During the late nineteen forties and early fifties, he translated the poetry of García Lorca, Brecht, Éluard, and Ungaretti, and wrote criticism, especially articles on surrealist art including pieces on Matisse, Picasso, Giacometti, and de Chirico. While living in Paris, he was associated with Breton, Éluard, Char, and others. Upon his return to Greece in 1953, he became a national figure in the cultural arena.

The poet would review the early part of that era in his only major prose statement on his art, *Open Papers* (a generous selection from *Open Papers* has been translated by Olga Broumas and T Begley, Copper Canyon Press, 1994). In "First Things First," he observes, "And yet from *what is* to *what could be*, you cross a bridge that takes you, no more, no less, from Hell to Paradise. And more bizarre: a Paradise composed of the exact same material as Hell. The only difference is our perception of the material's arrangement – understood by imagining it applied to ethical and emotional architectures.... This is the common qualifying trait characterizing the genus *poet*: dissent from current reality."

Labeled early as a Dionysian celebrant of ecstasy, he responds, "This is fundamentally wrong. I believe that poetry on a certain level of accomplishment is neither optimistic nor pessimistic. It represents rather a third state of the spirit where opposites cease to exist. There are no more opposites beyond a certain level of elevation. Such poetry is like nature itself, which is neither good nor bad, beautiful nor ugly; it simply *is*. Such poetry is no longer subject to habitual everyday distinctions.... The final goal of every exploration is inescapably nature. This, obviously, is very much part of the Hellenic tradition."

The mature work of Elytis is marked by his depth of knowledge, his use of the "old, pure Katharevousa" (an artificially constructed language based on Attic Greek), along with modern demotic Greek, local and regional dialect, multiple voices, neologisms, and structural harmonies drawing from the strophic/antistrophic composition of ancient liturgies and tragedies. And still his every chorus strives to achieve the realization of limpidity, the idea that within each image or idea is another complex image or idea, within which stand yet other images. His poetry amounts to a revelation of the working psyche as it becomes one with the poet's sense of commitment as he sings, in "Sun the First,"

> I give my hand to justice
> Transparent fountain source at the peak
> My sky is deep and unaltered
> What I love is always being born
> What I love is beginning always.

This, in the midst of World War II. If Kimon Friar's long out-of-print *The Sovereign Sun* was the best early general introduction to the poetry of Elytis, Olga Broumas's selection of his poems, *What I Love* (Copper Canyon Press, 1986), was the first to capture his lyric intensity.

The *Selected Poems*, edited and mostly translated by Edmund Keeley and Philip Sherrard (Viking Press / Penguin, 1981), was also a noble achievement. Considering the enormous complexity of this "poet of limpidity," he has been wonderfully served by his various translators, each with individual strengths.

Complexity and depth of perception are reflected even in the poet's *nom de plume*, which recalls such classical Greek themes and ideals as *Ellas* (Hellas), *elpídha* (hope), *eleftheria* (freedom), and of course *Eléni* (Helen). It also chooses a general rather than regional suffix to his surname. The poet nevertheless states, "Contrary to those who strive an entire life to 'fix' their literary likeness, I'm intent every hour and each moment on destroying mine, my face turned to proto-type alone, whose nature is to be endlessly created, ready to begin again precisely on account of life and art's oneness, which exists far before or after the sashaying of salons and of cafés." His conviction to keep "the mechanisms of myth-making but not the figures of mythol-ogy" is a poetic equivalent to the Confucian instruction, "Worship the virtue of ancestors, not ancestors themselves," and bears considerable moral as well as aesthetic weight.

The challenge to his translators lies in capturing his powerful lyric intensity without losing his inner "correspondences" within the im-agery, or stripping away his incantatory inventiveness. Just as we had to "go to school" on Pound and Eliot, H.D. and Williams, we must go to school on Elytis, "the most Greek of all Greek poets." For the American reader, ancient Greece – as interpreted through Roman classicism and the Italian Renaissance and Romantic poets from Eng-land – only gets in the way. As fellow Greek Nobel Poet George Seferis observed, modern Greek poets were forced "to destroy the traditional rationalism which lay heavily on the Western world" and "to regard Greek reality without the prejudices that have reigned since the Renaissance."

With publication of *The Axion Esti* in 1959, Elytis brought his mechanisms of mythmaking to full fruition in what translators Edmund Keeley and George Savidis have described as "a kind of spir-itual autobiography which attempts to dramatize the national and philosophical extensions of a highly personal sensibility. The poet's strategy – reminiscent of Whitman's in *Song of Myself* and Sikelianos's in *Prologue to Life* – is to present an image of the contemporary Greek consciousness through the developing perspective of a first-person persona who is at once the poet himself and the voice of his country." For this elaborate triptych, Elytis draws generously from the literary and historical Greece, including Homer, Heracleitos, and Pindar, from Byzantine hymnographers and Greek Orthodox liturgy, from folk songs and the autobiography of the great (and illiterate) General Makryannis. To translate a poem of such length – eighty pages of text – that is so intricately idiomatic and wrapped so snugly in Greek sound and rhythmic change is a nearly impossible task; and yet the Keeley / Savidis translation of *The Axion Esti* (University of Pittsburgh Press, 1974; presently out-of-print), achieves a maximum of poetry with few but excellent notes. It is a poem as monumental as Eliot's *Wasteland*, and probably the most widely read book of poetry in Greece since World War II, popularized in part by musical settings from the incomparable composer, Mikis Theodorakis. As much as anything else, *The Axion Esti* established Odysseas Elytis as a Nobel Prize candidate to be taken very seriously.

In a series of poems written concomitantly with *The Axion Esti* and published as *Six and One Remorses for the Sky* (1960), Elytis confronts the idea of Beauty in a world of evil and finds in his personification an otherly beauty in which is revealed the real landscape to be seen:

> Where, near the river, the dark ones fought against the
>   Angel, exactly showing how she's born, Beauty
>
> Or what we otherwise call tear.
>
> And long as her thinking lasted, you could feel it overflow
>   the glowing sight bitterly in the eyes and the huge, like
>   an ancient prostitute's, cheekbones
>
> Stretched to the extreme points of the Large Dog and of
>   the Virgin.
>
> "Far from the pestilential city I dreamed of her deserted
>   place where a tear may have no meaning and the only
>   light be from the flame that ravishes all that for me exists.

"Shoulder-to-shoulder under what will be, sworn to
   extreme silence and the co-ruling of the stars,

"As if I didn't know yet, the illiterate, that there exactly, in
   extreme silence are the most repellent thuds

"And that, since it became unbearable inside a man's chest,
   solitude dispersed and seeded stars!"

With the acknowledged loss of innocence (illiteracy), comes the
revelation of a deeper, truer landscape of the soul, mind solitary in its
awareness, and yet connected to the seeded stars. "Beauty" may indeed
be "otherly," she may stand alone in her "deserted place where a tear
may have no meaning," she nevertheless remains for the poet a palpa-
ble albeit inexplicable presence. A few years later, in "Villa Natacha,"
Elytis would say, "I have something to say transparent incomprehen-
sible / As birdsong in hour of war." And, "I dream a revolution on the
part of evil and of wars like that made on the part of chiaroscuro and
color shading, O Matisse."

He speaks for what insists upon remaining silent or unsayable. He
struggles to reveal a Paradise – not the dogma of eternal life hereafter,
but of a Paradise within, as though our inability to comprehend this
Paradise lay at the root of all human suffering, a tragedy of enormous
proportion, one that is itself the "other side" of Albert Camus's sense
of the absurd. Just as Camus was not an existentialist, Elytis is not a
surrealist. Both are Mediterranean preclassic sensibilities, each rep-
resenting a deep *humanitas*. While Elytis adores the moment of
innocence, his is a search for the awakening moment, for "enlighten-
ment," – in his own words, for the "drop of light in the vast night of
the soul." He remembers Matisse during the years of Auschwitz and
Buchenwald "painting the most juicy and ripe, the most charming
flowers and fruits which were ever made, as if the very miracle of life
had found a way to coil within them forever." The lost second lieu-
tenant of the Albanian campaign, the atrocities of war and the pesti-
lence of cities – nothing can destroy the Paradise within. "Let them
call me crazy / that out of nothing is born our Paradise."

In *Maria Nefele* (1978), he sets "parallel monologues" between
Maria, a kind of punk *bête noire* filled with the postadolescent ennui of

disillusionment, and an older male "Antiphonist," allowing "Maria of the Clouds" to become a figure for Helen, for Mary, and for Antigone, achieving the "limpidity" that has become a signature of his poetry, one figure seen within the next, with yet another within that. Maria excoriates "the poets," accusing them,

> What can I do with you my eyes the poets
> who years now pretend invincible souls
>
> And years wait for what I never did
> standing in line like unclaimed objects... (sic)
>
> What if they call you – not one of you answers
> outside the world's a mess everything burning
>
> Nothing you claim – I wish I knew with what brain –
> your rights in the vacuum!
>
> In times of wealth's worship o abandon
> you exude private property's vanity
>
> Wrapped up in Palm leaves you go on holding
> the wretched mourning-covered globe
>
> And in the stench of human sulfur you become
> the volunteer lab rats of the Holy.
>
> MAN'S PULLED BY GOD AS SHARK BY BLOOD.

The Antiphonist notes, "It is bigamy to love and to dream." And, "You 'fix' a truth exactly as you fix a lie."

Kimon Friar has written of Elytis's mature work, "He has kept to a strict demotic base with taste and discretion, but he has also added to his lexicon, grammar, syntax, and rhythmic embellishments taken from all periods of Greek literature.... Throughout his entire career he has been primarily interested in the plastic use of language, manipulating words and images like a painter or sculptor, shaping and reworking them as though they were colors or material. He has shaken off the tyranny of the speech of the common man, together with that of the pseudo-educated, which are both strangleholds on the creative spirit. He has returned to the language of the poet-saint, the prophet who must utter his vision in a common liturgy."

Elytis's major work since winning the 1979 Nobel Prize in Literature is the epic *The Little Mariner*, published in 1984 (translated by Olga Broumas, first published by Copper Canyon Press in 1988), another conceptual *tour de force* alternating prose poems with charged lyrical passages separated by four "spotlights" drawn from Greek history and personal mythology and three "catalogs" of influences from throughout the centuries. His lifelong search for an inner Paradise culminates near the end of *The Little Mariner* with the observation that "Yes, Paradise wasn't nostalgia. Nor, much less, a reward. It was a right." Like *The Axion Esti* before it, *The Little Mariner* bears the undeniable handprint of genius, of poetic authority, of visionary enlightenment.

Earlier, in *Open Papers*, he had warned, "Don't think me exalted; I'm not referring to myself; I speak for whoever feels as I do and is not naive enough to confess it. If a separate personal Paradise exists for each of us, I reckon mine must be irreparably planted with trees of words the wind silvers like poplars, by people who see their confiscated justice given back, and by birds that even in the midst of the truth of death insist on singing in Greek and saying, 'eros, eros, eros.'"

According to Hesiod, Eros is the first god to overcome humans *and* gods, and who instills within their souls all notions of beauty and anguish. Beauty and anguish, imagination and reality, Paradise and Hell – for Elytis, poetry, the truth of poetry, demolished such arbitrary distinctions, finding that "Paradise and Hell are made of exactly the same material." In Elytis's poetry, the major elements are air and water, both defined by light. "When I say 'Paradise,' I do not conceive of it in the Christian sense. It is another world which is incorporated into our own, and it is our fault that we are unable to grasp it." For the pre-Socratic imagination of Elytis, the *then* is found in the *now* just as the possible is seen within the impossible, the dream in the wakeful act.

On a visit to Athens nearly fifteen years ago, I went to see the poet in his modest apartment where he lived for fifty years, devoting his life to poetry, thanks to a small inheritance. Over a glass of Jack Daniels – "I've never cared for ouzo or retsina" – I explained that Olga Broumas's *What I Love*, which we were then planning to publish, would not bring him much money. Even a recent recipient of a Nobel Prize wouldn't sell more than a few thousands copies of poems in translation in the U.S.A. Then I asked about his Greek publisher.

"My publisher prints about 25,000 copies," he said. "and then, after a few weeks, when they're all sold, it's reprinted in paperback. But that doesn't matter," he added. "a *real* poet needs an audience of three. And since any poet worth his salt has two intelligent friends, one spends a lifetime searching for the third reader," he laughed. He had written in *Open Papers*, "*Trying not to lose even a moment of your supposed talent is like trying not to lose a cent of the interest on the small principal given you.* Poetry is not a bank. It is the antithesis, precisely. If a written text can be shared, so much the better. If not, it's all right. What must be practiced – assiduously, infinitely and without the slightest pause – is antiservitude, noncompliance, and independence. Poetry is the other face of Pride."

From among Elytis's last poems, Broumas has translated selections from *Outrock Elegies*, *The Garden with the Self-Deceptions*, and *West of Sorrow*, adding them to her previously published selections from all of Elytis's major works except *Axion Esti*. *Eros, Eros, Eros* draws from the same literary and spiritual traditions as Elytis's original Greek. Nobody but Olga Broumas, born in Greece and into the Sapphic tradition, could so embody the sound and movement and spirit of the original while bringing these poems into American English.

If the *Elegies* are a result of facing his own declining health, and immanent blindness and death, *West of Sorrow* represents a kind of transcendence, ultimately an expression of gratitude for that Paradise within. Composed while visiting Porto Rafti in 1995, a year before his death, the poems of *West of Sorrow* are the final testament of a great visionary. In "As Endymion," the last poem in his final suite of poems, he concludes:

> In a thousand sleeps one comes awake
> but it's forever.

Artemis Artemis grab me the moon's dog
It bites a cypress and unsettles the Eternals
Much deeper sleeps whom History has drenched
Light a match to its alcohol
                              it's only Poetry
Remains. Poetry. Just and essential and direct
As Adam and Eve imagined it – Just
In the pungent garden and infallible to clocks.

– *Sam Hamill*
  Kage-an, 1997

SOURCES:

Analogies of Light, edited by Ivar Ivask (University of Oklahoma Press, 1975).

49 Scholia on the Poems of Odysseas Elytis by Jeffrey Carson (Ypsilon Books, 1983).

Modern Greek Poetry by Edmund Keeley (Princeton University Press, 1983).

A version of this essay was originally published by *The Georgia Review*.

Eros, Eros, Eros
SELECTED AND LAST POEMS

What I Love

> Because tears are also
> Homeland that isn't lost
> There where they shone sometime later
> Truth arrived.

from the poem
Elytonesos, Commonly Elytisle

Sun the First

So often when I speak of the sun
In my tongue becomes tangled one
Large rose full of red.
But it is not bearable for me to be silent.

I   I don't know anymore the night terrible anonymity of death
In the small turn of my soul a fleet of stars comes to port.
Guard of evening because you shine next to the sky-colored
Little wind of an island that dreams of me
Proclaiming the dawn from its tall boulders
My two eyes embrace and sail you with the star
Of my correct heart: I don't know anymore the night.

I don't know anymore the names of a people that deny me
Clearly I read the shells the leaves the stars
Enmity is useless for me on the roads of the sky
Unless it is a dream that sees me once again
In tears walking through the sea of deathlessness
Evening under the curve of your golden fire
Night that is only night I do not know her.

II   BODY OF SUMMER

Time has gone since the last rain was heard
Over the ants and the lizards
Now sky burns without end
Fruit paint their mouth
Earth's pores open slowly slowly
And next to the water that drips syllabically
A huge plant looks the sun eye-to-eye!

Who is it lies on the high beaches
On his back toking silversmoked olive leaves
The cicadas are warmed in his ears

Ants work in his chest
Lizards slide in the grass of underarm
And from his feet's kelp a wave lightly passing
Sent by the young siren who sang:

O body of summer nude burnt
Eaten by oil and by salt
Body of boulder and shiver of heart
Large windblown of the hair tree-graceful
Basilbreath over the curly pubes
Full of small stars and fir needles
Body deep sailship of the day!

Slow rains come rapid hailstorms
Land slinks by whipped in the nails of the snow
That bruises in the depths with savage waves
The hills plunge in the clouds' thick teats

And yet behind it all you smile without care
And find again your immortal hour
As the sun on the beaches finds you again
As in your naked health the sun.

III   Day shiny shell of the voice you made me by
Naked to walk in my daily Sundays
Among the welcome of the shores
Blow the first-known wind
Spread out the greens of tenderness
So that the sun may loll his head
And light the poppies with his lips
The poppies that the proud will scythe
To keep no sign on their naked chest
But the blood of defiance that undoes sorrow
Arriving at the memory of freedom.

I spoke the love the health of the rose the ray
That alone directly finds the heart
Greece who with certainty steps on the sea
Greece who travels me always
On naked snow-glorious mountains.

I give my hand to justice
Transparent fountain source at the peak
My sky is deep and unaltered
What I love is always being born
What I love is beginning always.

iv   Drinking Corinthian sun
Reading the marbles
Climbing over the arbor seas
Targeting with the fishing spear
A covenant fish that slips
I found the leaves the sun's psalm has by heart
The live dry land desire rejoices
To open.

I drink water I cut fruit
I shove my hand in the leafy wind
The lemon trees irrigate the pollen of summer
Green birds tear my dreams
I leave in a glance
Eyes wide where the world becomes again
Beautiful from the beginning to the measurement of the heart.

The Hyacinth Symphony

I   Stand a little closer to the silence and gather the hair of this night dreaming her naked body. It has many horizons, many composers, and a fate that burns tirelessly each time all fifty-two of her cards. Then she begins with something else – your hand, to which she gives pearls so it may find a desire, an inlet of sleep.

Stand a little closer to the silence and embrace the huge anchor that regales the depths. Soon, in the clouds. And you will not understand, but cry, cry for me to kiss you, and when I go to open a slit in the lie, a small blue skylight in intoxication, you'll bite me. Small, jealous of my soul shadow, breeder of a music under the moon.

Stand a little closer to me.

IV   Five swallows – five words with you as a destination. Each flash closes on you. Before becoming simplified as grass you leave your shape on a rock painfully waving its flames toward the interior. Before becoming a taste of loneliness you wrap the thyme shrubs in memories.

And I, I arrive always directly at absence. One sound makes the creek and what I say, what I love remains untouched in its shadows. Innocence and pebbles in clarity's depth. Crystal sensation.

VII   Emotion. The leaves tremble living together and living apart on the poplars sharing the wind. Before your eyes one sets free memories, these pebbles – chimeras! Time is fluid and you steady on it, acanthine. I consider those who never accepted life vests. Who love the light under the lids, who with sleep in midheaven sleeplessly study their open hands.

And I want to close the circles opened by your own fingers, to fit the sky on them so that their final word never be other.

Speak to me but speak of tears.

x　　Once more among the cherry trees your hard-found lips. Once more among the vegetable swings your ancient dreams. Once, in your ancient dreams, the songs that light up and vanish. In those that light up and vanish the world's warm mysteries. The world's secrets.

xiv　　You return to the pumice island with a short forgotten hymn that resurrects the bells, giving a matutinal dome to your most expatriate memories. You shake the small gardens from your heart and then again help yourself to their sorrow. You feel nothing above the severe boulders and yet suddenly your form resembles their singing. The irregular stone steps take you high, high and there are your heartbeats outside the gate of the new. You gather laurel and marble for the white architecture of your luck.

And you are as you were born, the world's center.

xvii　　You learned nothing from what was born and died under the desires. You won the confidence of a life that didn't tame you and you continue the dream. What can things say, and which ones scorn you!

When you flash in the sun that on you shines liquid and immortal hyacinths and silences, I name you single reality. When you rescue the dark and return with dawn, spring, bud, ray, I name you single reality. When you leave those who assimilate nonexistence and offer yourself human, I wake from the beginning in your change...

Play no more. Throw the ace of fire. Open the human geography.

xxi　　You have a mortal earth whose leaves you count endlessly and do not sleep. So many hills, you say, so many seas, such flowers. And your one heart becomes plural idealizing their fifth essence. And wherever you go space opens and what word you send out to infinity embraces me. Guess, work, feel:

From the other side I am the same.

Famous Night

… by the terraces, near the musical complaint of your hand's curve. Near your transparent breast, the uncovered forests full of violets and vegetables and open palms of moon, far as the sea, the sea you caress, the sea that takes and leaves me leaving in a thousand shells.

Visible and beautiful I taste your good moment! I say that you communicate so well with people you raise them to the dimension of your heart so none again can worship what belongs to him, what stirs like a tear at the root of every grass, the crown of each reached branch. I say that you communicate so well with the spring of things that your fingers match their fate. Visible and beautiful by your side I am whole! I want boundless paths at the crossroads of birds and of fair people, the gathering of stars that will co-rule. And I want to touch something, even your smallest firefly unsuspiciously jumping in the field's mane, so I can write with certain fire that nothing is transient in the world since the moment we chose, this moment we want over and above the all-gold contrariety, over and above the calamity of death's frost, in the path of each wind with love sighting our heart, in the superb gooseflesh of the sky that day and night is kneaded by the goodness of stars.

Ode to Picasso

1   As when
          having set fire to a fuse of hemp
The quarrymen run away
Signaling like crazy
And a volley of wind suddenly down the ravine drags their straw hats
As when
          a violin all alone raves in the dark
And the lover's melancholy heart spreads its Asia
The poppies in the grenade's flash
The stone hands immobile in the desert and terrible pointing
          always the same way
Calling
Meaning
Life's no hermitage
Life can't bear silence
With hot springs and avalanches it rises or rolls murmuring lovewords
Words that whatever they say never lie
Words that begin as birds and arrive "flaming ethyl"
Because the world doesn't have two elements – is not divisible
Pablo Picasso – and joy as grief on a human brow
Juego de luna y arena – meet where sleep
Lets bodies speak – where you draw
Death or Love
Nude and defenseless alike under the North's terrible nostrils
AS ONLY THEN YOU EXIST.

Truly Picasso Pablo you exist
And with you we exist
Ceaselessly they build black stones around us but you laugh
Black walls around us – but you at once
Open on them a myriad doors and windows
To spill in the sun that oh! fireblond scream
Enlarging and proclaiming passionately in love the gasses liquids
          solids of this earth

So that nothing battles another
No one battles another
No enemy exists
And side by side the lamb walks with the lion
And life like a Guadalquivir of stars my brother
Tumbles down clear water and gold
A thousand leagues into its dreams
A thousand leagues into our dreams…

II   So the knife enters flesh – and the breath of warm bread so rises. Also
The tall oak's creaking
On mountains thunder respects – and also
The multitudes on the piazza storming with red bandannas the first
        of May –
Your large black eyes heatwave the world
The Mediterranean suns itself in them and the wild boulder goats
        crane their rough necks
Windfall –
Your broad hairy breasts a sulphured vineyard
A mythic insect your right hand
Coming and going on white papers in shadow and light
Comes and goes buzzing
Rouses colors and shapes
Not only what the housewives put up on shelves for the great
        Sabbath
Honeymoon memories
All golden sequins and rosy rhombs
But also those others one can see when taken by a deep duende
In children's prams
In the horse-carriages' double springs
In turtles' eggs
In vipers thrashing on fire
Or in the continents' infinite forests still
– Night falling –
When cross-legged round the fire Negroes chant all at once
        "Hallelujah" with mouth harps

What doesn't burn them – what endures
On life's large plateaus on lost Aztec memorials
On the waning moon the full acanthine sun – what's unspeakable
And yet in moments of superabundant godliness revealed
Picasso: stubborn as the magnetic needle's North turn
Picasso: steel burns in foundries
Picasso: an armored warship disappears in the deep
Picasso: disproportion of surrealistic flora
Picasso: good summary of a kilometer-long sail
Picasso: Paloma
Picasso: Centaur
Picasso: Guernica.

III A proud heart vanquishes black darkness – and cuts the Gordian
                bond of things a rapier the proud heart
A fabulous thing humankind if you but think
The hay bending the sky
Is the girl looking her lover in the eye
Is the young girl's "I love you"
At the hour when large cities
Turning slowly on their axle
Show square windows ill-lit
Remains of old-timers with triangular heads rotating their one eye
Stairs on stairs corridors on corridors
DANGER
NO EXIT
DISALLOWED
Half horseman the kidnapper gallops – and the giant-soled
                woman stretches
In the air her horizontal arms
Bitter years past Christ
But for a little heart the world would be different
Different the chapel of the earth
But there! the Good Samaritan weeps forgotten tying an ancient
                dragon root at his feet

At the hour when you beast
You Pablo Picasso
Picasso Pablo fit in your wiltless eye
What God can't in a million planted acres
You work your brush like singing
Like caressing wolves or swallowing conflagrations
Like night and day with a nymphomaniac
Like throwing orange peels in the middle of a feast
While you
Stormkissed Pablo Picasso seize Death by the wrists
And wrestle him a beautiful wellborn Minotaur
What he spills in blood you draw in courage
You take pass leave take up again
Flowers animals embraces aromas dungs boulders diamonds
To equalize them in infinity the same motion of earth that brought
and takes us
You draw for you and me
You draw for all my comrades
You draw for all the years that passed and pass and will pass still.

Beauty and the Illiterate

Often, in the Repose of Evening her soul took a lightness from
        the mountains across, although the day was harsh and
        tomorrow foreign.

But, when it darkened well and out came the priest's hand over
        the little garden of the dead, She

Alone, Standing, with the few domestics of the night – the blowing
        rosemary and the murmur of smoke from the kilns –
        at sea's entry, wakeful

Otherly beauty!

Only the waves' words half-guessed or in a rustle, and others
        resembling the dead's that startle in the cypress, strange
        zodiacs that lit up her magnetic moon-turned head.
        And one

Unbelievable cleanliness allowed, to great depth in her, the real
        landscape to be seen,

Where, near the river, the dark ones fought against the Angel,
        exactly showing how she's born, Beauty

Or what we otherwise call tear.

And long as her thinking lasted, you could feel it overflow the
        glowing sight bitterly in the eyes and the huge, like an
        ancient prostitute's, cheekbones

Stretched to the extreme points of the Large Dog and of the Virgin.

"Far from the pestilential city I dreamed of her deserted place
where a tear may have no meaning and the only light be
from the flame that ravishes all that for me exists.

"Shoulder-to-shoulder under what will be, sworn to extreme silence
and the co-ruling of the stars,

"As if I didn't know yet, the illiterate, that there exactly, in extreme
silence are the most repellent thuds

"And that, since it became unbearable inside a man's chest, solitude
dispersed and seeded stars!"

Daughter the North Wind Was Bringing

Far inside the smell of doublemint I reconsidered where I was going
and I said so as not to be at the mercy of the wild   find a small
church to have a talk.

The lowing of the pelago ate like a she-goat my black gut and left
an opening increasingly calling to the joys   But nothing   no one

Just fiery all around the intuition of wild olive

And the entire   the length of the foamdust   high over my head
hillside   prophesied and murmured   with a myriad purple tremors
and cherubic insects   Yes yes I agreed   these seas will take revenge
ONE DAY THESE SEAS WILL TAKE REVENGE.

Until   up there   detached from her ruins she appeared gaining in
height   and beautiful beyond addition with all the birds' habits in
her sway   daughter the north wind was bringing and I waiting

Each fathom forward   as she flung a small breast to resist the wind
and from inside me a terrified happiness raising its wing to my lids

Ai! tempers and madness of my land!

Behind her fans of light broke leaving in the sky something like
signs untouched from Paradise

I was able momentarily to see   the fork of legs enlarged   the
whole inner part   with the little still saliva of the sea   Then her
smell came to me   all fresh bread and wild mallow

I pushed the small wood door and lit a candle
That an idea of mine had come immortal.

Small Green Sea

Small green sea thirteen years old
I want to adopt you
Send you to school in Ionia
To learn of mandarin and of absinthe
Small green sea thirteen years old
In the tight tower of the lighthouse at noon
Turn to the sun and hear
How fate's undone and how
From hill to hill still
Our distant relations who hold
The wind like statues communicate
Small green sea thirteen years old
With the white collar and the ribbon
Go through Smyrna's window
And copy the light reflected on the ceilings
From the Lordhavemercies and the Glorybe
And with a little north a little levantine
Wave by wave come back
Small green sea thirteen years old
Illegally to me to sleep
To find deep in your keep
Pieces of stone the talk of Gods
Pieces of Stone Heracleitos's fragments.

Villa Natacha

I have something to say transparent incomprehensible
As birdsong in hour of war.

Here, in a corner where I sat
To smoke my first free cigarette
Awkward in happiness, trembling
If I should break a flower, offend some bird
And in a difficult position, on my behalf, God find himself

And yet they all obey me
The straight bamboo and the bowing belfry
And the garden's anchorage complete
Countermirrored in my mind
One by one the names that sound
Strange in the foreign tongue: *Phlox, Aster, Cytise*
Eglantine, Pervenche, Colchique
Alise, Frésia, Pivoine, Myoprone
Muguet, Bleuet
Saxifrage
Iris, Clochette, Myosotis
Primevère, Aubépine, Tubereuse
Paquerette, Ancolie, and the shapes all
Clearly written in the fruit: the circle, the square
The triangle and rhombus
As the birds see them, let the world be made simple
A Picasso design
With woman, child and seahorse.

I say: this too will come. Something else pass.
Much is not wanted by the world. One something
Minute. Like the crooked steering before the accident
But
Exactly

To
The opposite direction

Enough we've worshiped danger and it's the season it paid us back.

I dream a revolution on the part of evil and of wars like that made on the part of chiaroscuro and color shading, O Matisse.

The Monogram

I'll mourn always – you hear me? – for you,
alone, in Paradise.

I   Fate will turn elsewhere the engravings
Of the palm, like a key keeper
Some moment Time will acquiesce

How else, since people love each other

The sky will represent our guts
And innocence will smite the world
With black death's acrid sickle.

II   I mourn the sun and I mourn the years that come
Without us and I sing those others gone
If it's true

That bodies conspired with the boats struck sweetly
The guitars flickering under the waters
The *believe me* and the *don't*
Once in the air, once in the music

The two small animals, our hands
That looked to climb secretly one on the other
The pot of coolweed in the open yards
And the seas in pieces coming together
Over the dryrock, behind the fence
The anemone that sat in your hand
And trembled three times purple three days above the falls

If these are true I sing
The wooden beam and the square weaving
On the wall, the Mermaid with unplaited hair
The cat who saw us in the dark

Child with frankincense and red cross
In the hour of dusk by the unapproachable boulders
I mourn the garment I touched and the world came to me.

III   This is how I speak for you and me

Because I love you and in love I know
Like a Full Moon to enter
From everywhere, for your small foot in the vast sheets
I unpetal jasmines – and I have the strength
Asleep, to blow and take you
Through luminous passages and the sea's secret arcades
Hypnotized trees silver with spiders

The waves have heard of you
How you caress, how you kiss
How you whisper *what* and *eh*
Around the neck the bay
Always we the light and shade

Always you little star and always I dark navigable
Always you the port and I the lantern at right
The wet mooring and the oar's shine
High in the house with the grape arbor
The tied roses, the water that cools
Always you the stone statue and always I shade that grows
The pulled shutter you, the wind that opens it I
Because I love you and I love you
Always you the coin and I the worship that cashes it:

So much the night, so much the howl in the wind
So much the dew in the air, so much for silence
Around us the despotic sea
Arc of the sky with stars
So much your least breath

That at last I've nothing left
In the four walls, the ceiling, the floor
To call on but you and my voice beats me
To smell of but you and people go wild
Because the untried and the from elsewhere brought
Are intolerable and it's early, do you hear me
It is early still in this world my love

To speak about you and about me.

IV   It is still early in this world, do you hear me
The beasts have not been tamed, do you hear me
My spilled blood and the pointed, do you hear me
Knife
Like a ram running the skies
Snapping the stars' branches, do you hear me
It's me, do you hear me
I love you, do you hear me
I hold you and take you and dress you
In Ophelia's white bridal, do you hear me
Where do you leave me, where do you go and who, do you hear me

Holds your hands over the floods

The enormous lianas and the volcanoes' lavas
One day, do you hear me
Will bury us and the thousand later years, do you hear
Luminous will make of us strata, do you hear me
On which the heartlessness of, do you hear me
People will shine
And throw us a thousand pieces, do you hear
In the water one by one, do you hear
I count my bitter pebbles, do you hear me
And time is a large church, do you hear

Where sometimes the figures, do you hear me
Of Saints
Emit a real tear, do you hear
The bells open on high, do you hear me
A passage deep for me to pass
The angels wait with candles and funereal psalms
I am not going anywhere, do you hear me
Either neither or together both, do you hear me

This flower of storm and, do you hear
Of love
We cut once and for all, do you hear me
And it can't flower otherwise, do you hear me
In another earth, another star, do you hear me
The soil is gone, the air is gone
That we touched, that same, do you hear me

And no gardener ever had the luck

From so much winter so much north wind, do you hear me
To pull a flower, only we, do you hear me
In the middle of the sea
From just the wanting of love, do you hear me
Raised a whole island, do you hear
With caves and coves and flowering gullies
Hear, hear
Who speaks to the waters and who cries – hear?
Who looks for the other, who shouts – hear?
It's me who shouts and it's me who cries, do you hear me
I love you, I love you, you hear me.

v   Of you I've spoken long ago
With wise nurses and veteran rebels
What gives you the sorrow of a beast
On your face the trembling water's reflection
And why am I meant to come near you

I who don't want love but want the wind
Want the uncovered standing sea's full gallop

And none had heard of you
Not the doubleroot and not the mushroom
In Crete's high places nothing
Of you but God accepted to guide my hand

A little here, a little there, carefully the whole circle
Of the beach, the face, the bay, the hair
Of the hill waving toward the left

Your body in the stance of the solitary plane tree
Eyes of pride and the transparent
Seafloor, in the house with the old screen
The yellow lace and cypresswood
I wait for you alone to first appear
High in the room or behind the flagstones
With the Saint's horse and the Easter egg

As if from a destroyed fresco
Large as small life wanted you
To fit inside a candle the stentorian volcanic flash

So no one might have seen nor heard
Anything in the deserts the ruined houses
About you, not the ancestor buried at yard's edge
Nor the old crone with all her herbs

About you only I, maybe, and the music
I chase from me but stronger it returns
For you the unformed twelve-year-old breast
Turned to the future with its red crater
For you the bitter odor like a pin
That in the body finds and pierces memory
And there's the soil, there doves, there our ancient earth.

VI   I've seen a lot and the earth, to my mind, is more beautiful
More beautiful in the golden vapors
The cutting stone, more beautiful
The isthmus purple and the roofs like waves
The rays more beautiful where without stepping you pass
Invincible like the goddess of Samothrace over the mountainous sea

I've seen you so and it's enough
That all time's been absolved
In the small channel your passing leaves
Like a novice dolphin following

And playing with the white and the cyanic blue my soul!

Victory, victory where I've been beaten
Before love and with love
To passion flowers and mimosa
Go, go, even if I am lost

Alone, though the sun you hold is a newborn
Alone, though I'm the homeland that mourns
Though the word I sent to hold a laurel to you is
Alone, the wind strong and alone
In the blink of the dark seafloor the pebble
Paradise
The fisherman lifted and threw back again at Time.

VII   In Paradise I've sighted an island
Identical you and a house by the sea

With a big bed and a small door
I've thrown an echo to the deep
To see myself each morning waking

To see you half passing in the water
And weep for you half in Paradise.

Selections from

Maria Nefele

Guess, work, feel: From the other side
I am the same.

The Presence

MARIA NEFELE:

I walk in thorns in the dark
of what's to happen and what has
with my only weapon my only defense
my nails purple like cyclamens.

ANTIPHONIST:

I saw her everywhere. Holding a glass and staring into space. Lying
down listening to records. Walking the streets in wide trousers and an
old gabardine. In front of children's-store windows. Sadder then. And
in discotheques, more nervous, eating her nails. She smokes innumer-
able cigarettes. She is pale and beautiful. But if you talk to her she
doesn't hear at all. As if something is happening – she alone hears it
and is frightened. She holds your hand tight, tears, but is not *there*. I
never touched her and I never took from her anything.

MN: He understood nothing. He kept asking all the time "Remember?"
What's to remember? My dreams alone I remember because I see
them at night. Days I feel bad – how to say: unprepared. I found
myself so suddenly, in life – where I'd hardly expected. I'd say "Bah,
I'll get used to it." And everything around me ran. Things and people
ran, ran – until I set myself to run like crazy. But, it seems, I overdid.
Because – I don't know – something strange happened in the end.
First I'd see the corpse and then the murder. First came the blood and
then the blow and cry. And now, when I hear rain I don't know
what's waiting…

A: "Why don't they bury people standing up like archbishops?" – that's
what she'd say to me. And once, I remember, summer on the island,
all of us coming from a party, dawn, we jumped over the bars of the
museum's garden. She danced on the stones and she saw nothing.

MN: I saw his eyes. I saw some old olive groves.

29

A: I saw a column on a grave. A girl in relief on the stone. She seemed sad and held a small bird in her cupped hand.

MN: He was looking at me, I know, he was looking at me. We both were looking at the same stone. We looked at each other through the stone.

A: She was calm and in her palm she held a small bird.

MN: She was sitting and she was dead.

A: She was sitting and in her palm she held a small bird. You'll never hold a bird like that – you aren't able.

MN: Oh if they let me, if they let me.

A: If who let you?

MN: The one who lets nothing.

A: He, he who lets nothing
      is cut by his shadow and walks away.

MN: His words are white and unspeakable
      his eyes deep and without sleep...

A: But the whole upper part of the stone was taken. And with it her name.

MN: ARIMNA – as if I could still see the letters carved inside the light...
      ARIMNA EFE EL...

A: Gone. The whole top gone. There were no letters at all.

MN: ARIMNA EFE EL – there, on that EL the stone had cut and broken. I remember it well.

A: She must have seen it in a dream since she remembers.

MN: In my dream, yes. In a large sleep that will come sometime all light and heat and small stony steps. The children will walk in the streets arm in arm like in some old Italian movies. Song everywhere and enormous women in small balconies watering their flowers.

A: A large blue balloon will take us high then, here and there, the wind will beat us. The silver domes will stand out first, then the bellfries. The streets will appear narrower and straighter than we imagined. The terraces with the white television antennas. And all around the hills, and the kites – so close we'll just shave past them. Until one moment we'll see the whole sea. On it the souls will be leaving small white steams.

MN: I have lifted my hand against the mountains, the dark and the demonic of this world. I've asked love "Why?" and rolled her on the floor. War and war and not one rag to hide deep in our things and forget. Who listens? Who listened? Judges, priests, police, which is your country? One body is left me and I give it. On it those who know cultivate the holy, as the gardeners in Holland, tulips. And in it drown who never learned of sea or swimming... Flux of the sea and you stars' distant influx – stand by me!

A: I have lifted my hand against the
unexorcised demons of the world
and from the place of illness I have exited
to the sun and to the light self-exiled!

MN: And from too many storms I've exited
self among humans exiled!

What Convinces

Please pay attention to my lips: from them the world depends.
From the associations they risk and the unacceptable
similes as when one fragrant night
we throw the Moon's woodcutter down
he bribes us with a little jasmine and we acquiesce...

What convinces I maintain is like the chemical substance
                that transmutes.
Let the cheek of a girl be beautiful
all of us with eaten faces will return someday from the Truthsites.

Folks I can't explain it
but it's time to understudy the old Robbers.
To stretch our hand and have it go
where a woman like an apple tree waits half a day in the clouds
ignoring completely the distance that parts us.

And something else: when it starts to rain
let us undress and shine like clover.

WRONG SEA IS IMPOSSIBLE.

MARIA NEFELE:

The Poets

What can I do with you my eyes the poets
who years now pretend invincible souls

And years wait for what I never did
standing in line like unclaimed objects…

What if they call you – not one of you answers
outside the world's a mess everything burning

Nothing you claim – I wish I knew with what brain –
your rights in the vacuum!

In times of wealth's worship o abandon
you exude private property's vanity

Wrapped up in Palm leaves you go on holding
the wretched mourning-covered globe

And in the stench of human sulphur you become
the volunteer lab rats of the Holy.

MAN'S PULLED BY GOD AS SHARK BY BLOOD.

Helen

Maria Nefele doubtlessly
is a sharp girl
a true threat of the future;
sometimes she shines like a knife
and a drop of blood on her
has the significance that another time
the L of the Iliad had.

Maria Nefele goes forth
liberated from the abhorred notion of the eternal cycle.

With her existence alone
she annihilates half the people.

Maria Nefele lives at the antipodes of Ethics
she is all habit.

When she says "I'll sleep with him,"
she means she'll kill history one more time.
One must see then what enthusiasm overtakes the birds.

Besides in her manner
she perpetuates the olive's nature.
She becomes according to the moment
now silver now deeply blue.

And that's why adversaries continuously
march – look:
some with their social theories
many simply brandishing flowers

Every time and its Helen.

FROM YOUR REFLECTION SUN CONGEALS INSIDE THE
POMEGRANATE AND REJOICES.

Maria Nefele's Song

"What a waste of a girl," they say
shake their heads
like it's for me they worry
I wish they'd buzz off!

I cruise the clouds
like the beautiful lightning
and what I give and take
turns to rain.

Hey look at me guys
I cut on both sides
mornings I can't be talked to
curse Marys

nights I roll
on anybody's lawn
as if polestruck
drunga-drunga-drung.

I haven't met joy
and I step on grief
like an angel I turn
over the ravine.

The Nefelegerétes
(who gathers clouds)

Ah how beautiful to hang out with the clouds
to write like Homer epics on old shoes
to not care if you're liked or not
nothing

Free of distraction to reap unpopularity
like this; with generosity; as if you owned
a mint and shut it
fired all personnel
to keep a poverty had by no other
completely yours.
At the hour when at their bureaus without hope
hanging by phones
they fight for nothing the fat people
you go up inside Eros
totally smudged but limber
a chimney sweep
you come down from Eros ready to found
your own white beach

without money

you undress as they who know of stars undress
and with large leagues open yourself freely to cry...

IT IS BIGAMY TO LOVE AND TO DREAM.

The Kite

And yet I was meant to be a kite.
I liked heights even when
I stayed on my pillow face down
punished
hours and hours.
I felt my room rose
I wasn't dreaming – rose
I was scared and I liked it.
What I saw was how to say
something like a "remembrance of the future"
all trees departing mountains changing face
geometric fields with small curly forests
like pubes – I was scared and I liked it
barely touching the bellfries
caressing their bells like balls and getting lost…

People with light umbrellas ambled by on an angle
and smiled at me;
sometimes they rapped on the window: "Miss"
I was scared and I liked it.
They were the "up people" that's what I called them
they weren't like the "down";
they had beards and many held in hand a gardenia;
some half-opened the balcony door
and put strange records on the hi-fi.
There was I remember "Annetta with Sandals"
"The Geyser of Spitsburgh"
the "Fruit We Didn't Bite May Won't Visit Us"
(yes I remember others)
I say it again – I wasn't dreaming
suddenly that "Half-part Your Garment and I Have a Bird for You."
The bicycle knight had brought it

one day I was sitting pretending to read
with extreme attention he had leaned
his bicycle next to my bed;
then he pulled the string and I engulfed the air
my colored underthings were shining
I was watching how transparent those who love become
tropical fruit and kerchiefs of distant continents;
I was scared and I liked it.
My room rose
or I – I never understood it.
I of porcelain and magnolia
my hand descends from the most ancient Inca
I slip between doors as
an infinitesimal earthquake
felt only by infants and dogs;
by necessity I must be a monster
and yet opposition
has always nourished me and that remains
for those with pointed hats
who converse secretly with my mother
at night to solve. Sometimes
the trumpet-cry from the distant barracks
unraveled me like a streamer and everyone around
was clapping – disbelieved years in fragments
suspended in the air.
In the bath next door the faucets open
face down on my pillow
I watched the immaculate white fountains splashing me;
how beautiful my God how beautiful
foot-trampled on the ground
to still hold in my eyes
such mourning for the distant past.

INSIDE AND OUT IMAGINATION'S WORN AND IN ALL HER SIZES.

The Forefathers' Paradise

I don't know shit about forefathers' sins
and other Western inventions.
But really there away
in the dew of the first days
before our mother's hut
how beautiful it was.

The angels' whites as I recall them
closed in the front but were left unbuttoned
just like the overalls of girls working in salons
fabulous – and all the geraniums
on a long whitewashed flagstone
turned to the wind you could see them milling
ceaselessly the black bread of the sun.

Fresh days in umbra and in sienna
when the island seemed a boundless Lassithi
weightless and just cast
on a dazzling shattered sea.

One leg over the other
on the beach ridged by the wind
all gold sparks from spurs
galloping I watched I remember
sirocco girls with cool thighs
unwinding a hair like clover;
and my heart against the naked mountains across
dook-dook counterechoed like a motor schooner.

It was the time of Leaf and Shiny
when Seth and Merione ruled.

Nights I had meaning – I gave it to the nightingales
and sleep was sweet full of half-moons
brooks in c major for viola d'amore.

There were daisies you ate
and others that lit up in the dark like fireworks;
the vast grass groaned and made the love;
under your feet passed stars
like flocks of fish and the cove
deep blue advanced in your entrails –
how good it was!

The angels teased me; often
gathered around me they'd ask:
"What's pain?" and "What's illness?" and I didn't know at all.
I didn't know I hadn't even heard about
the Tree from where death entered
the world. So? Was death true? Not him – the other
who comes in the newborn's cry? Was it true
injustice? That nations' mania? Night and day toil?

Downwind of herbs I sucked in basil
and all the archangels Michael Gabriel
Uriel Raphael
Gabudel Achir Ariukh
Belial Zabuleon laughed stirring
their golden heads like corn;
knowing the only death the only one is that
which people made up with their minds

And their great lie the Tree did not exist.

YOU "FIX" A TRUTH EXACTLY AS YOU FIX A LIE.

Patmos

Before you meet death changes you;
alive still with his fingermarks
on us half-wild hair agitated we bend
gesturing over incomprehensible harps. But
the world leaves…
Ai ai the beautiful can't happen twice
nor love.

Too bad world too bad
the future dead rule you
and no one no one's had the chance
chance yet to hear
not one voice of angels nor waters
nor that "come" that in nights of great insomnia I dreamt.

There there I go on a loose-rocked island
the sun treads on crookedly like the crab
and the entire trembling basin of the sea listens and calls back.

Armed fully with sixteen baggages sleeping bags maps
plastic sacks tape measures and teleoptic lenses
crates of bottled mineral water
I set out – the second time – and nothing.

Already nine o'clock on Mykonos pier
erased among the ouzo and the English
habitué of a weightless sky where all
things weigh twice their weight
while the umbilical stretches from the stars
to break and you're lost…

I slept as only one can sleep
on a bed warmed by the backs of others

I was walking rather on a deserted shore
where the moon hemorrhaged and you heard nothing but
the wind's steps on the rotten wood.
Up to the knee in the water I took to glowing
from inside me a strange gusto
I opened my legs
slowly slowly my guts began
mauve cyanic orange to fall;
tenderly bending I washed them one by one
carefully especially the parts I saw
left with lesions where the Invisible had bit.

Until I gathered them all in my apron
without walking I advanced
the music blew and pushed me
pieces of sea here – pieces of sea farther on.
My God where does one go without a fate
where without star
empty sky empty body
and only bitterness round full
inside the half-moon stirring her thorns
one more you can never touch
female urchin.

Right there I woke in the strange house;
my hand groping in the dark
across the nail scissors found the sharp
break in the continuity of the skin
the sharp break in the world's continuity.
Here loss – there salvation.
Here mercurochrome tensoplast
there the beast hungry in the deserts
howling biting
dragging the sun through the fumes.

WHEN YOU HEAR WIND IT'S CALM TURNED VAMPIRE.

Pax San Tropezana

What a great cow earth's become these days!
Walks on all fours breathing heavily with joy
gee-up!
Glory be to the established fathers
peace reigns
small and large animals there by ship traverse…

Painted tits two-tone pants
oversize straw hats of all fashion
coats of arms of rich princes aspiring masochists
authors by distance
twenty-four-hour actors
they piss in the sea and emit small cries
Mix-European
ou-ou ou-ou!

High in the sky black voids
gape and the odor
of souls lets a thick-flowing smoke escape.
Occasionally a Saint's gaze appears clearly
fierce as never
"there is no meaning meaning is elsewhere"
colored and felt-up the multitudes go on
with half-closed eyes like toddlers crawling
gee-up!
Pax
Pax San Tropezana
peace reigns.
Mix-European everything gets said
gets done undone
with easy terms and installments.
Time of spare parts

bust a tire – change a tire
lose a Jimmy – find a Bob
c'est très pratique as Annette would say
the beautiful waitress of *Tahiti*.
Her breasts were autographed by nineteen lovers
together with their place of birth
a small tender geography.

But I think deep down she was a homosexual.

EAT PROGRESS WITH HER PEELINGS AND PIPS.

Electra Bar

Two or three steps below the surface
of the earth – and all your problems solved directly!
You hold the small world in a large crystal glass;
through ice cubes you see your colored nails
faces that smile indefinitely;
you see your Luck (but always with her back turned, her)
Virago that crossed you and you never revenged…

Ah Erica was right
the flying stewardess of Olympic
she passes high above the capitals;
I must pass below them – below the fat fed bodies
if I can ever achieve (and again that's debatable)
that vein where Agamemnon's blood still flows
without other help other unknown brother –

Give me another gin fizz.

It's so lovely when the mind clouds – there heroes kill
make-believe like in the movies
you get your fill of blood; at the hour when the real thing
gurgles down the stairs
you touch a finger and wake the curse
the Queen with spiders
her eyes unbeaten and full of dark
shorn and ugly I pasture swine
eons now outside the walls
I wait for the message – the first cock in Hell
something like the saxophone with a heavenly gloss
like young girls running riding dragons of rubber.

Earth only now revealed how great in reality.
Zeus thunders
blackness
Zeus thunders
neither defeat nor victory this.

Let's risk something else, we, the interred.

WHO CHARGES SOLITUDE STILL HAS HUMANS INSIDE HIM.

The Apocalypse

Narrow the road – the wide I never knew
unless just once
then when I kissed you hearing the sea…

And it's from then I speak – it is the same sea
reaching into my sleep that ate hard stone
and opened borderless. I learned words
like a passage of green fish
with blue chalk inscribed
sleeptalk that I unlearned awake
and swimming again felt and interpreted
John of the loves
face down
on the blankets of a bed in a provincial hotel
with the bulb naked at the end of the wire
and the black cockroach stopped on the sink.
To what to what to be human
the luxury grade in the animal world
what can it mean
except if you have ears hear
don't fear what you will have to feel.

I didn't fear
I not at all humbly however endured
I saw death three times
I they threw me from the doors outside.

If you have ears hear. I heard
a roar as from a pelagic shell
and turning in the light suddenly saw
four dark-in-the-face boys
that blew and pushed pushed and brought

a piece of thin earth belted in drystone
all in all seven olive trees
and among them old he seemed the goatherd
his foot unsandaled on the stone.

"It's me," he said "don't be afraid
of what is written you to feel."
And stretching out his right hand
showed me in his palm the seven deep entrenchments:
"These are the great sorrows
and these will be written on your face
though I'll erase for you with this same hand
that brought them."

And at once behind his hand I saw – it appeared
a mob of many men speechless from fear
who cried and ran ran and squealed
"There comes Avathon there comes the Releaser."
I felt great turbulence and anger
mastered me. But he himself went on:
"Let who cheated cheat still. And the filthy
be filthier. And the just
more just let be." And because I sighed
with endless serenity he stretched his hand
slowly on my face
and it was sweet as honey but it embittered my gut.

"You must again prophesy to peoples and nations
and tongues and many kings,"
he said; and shooting white flames joined the sun.

Such my first dream that still
I cannot part it from the voices of the sea
and save it clean.
It can't be done in words the dream.

My lie so real
My lips burn still.

IF YOU DON'T FIX YOUR FOOT OUTSIDE THE EARTH YOU'LL NEVER
MAKE IT STAY ON HER.

The Little Mariner

Entrance

SOMETIMES IT'S NOTHING BUT

a flash behind the mountains – there, by the island-littered sea.
Sometimes again a strong wind suddenly stops outside the harbors.
And those who understand grow tearful

Gold wind of life why don't you reach us?

No one hears, no one. Everyone walks with an icon, and on it, fire.
And not a day, a moment in this place without injustice, murder

Why don't you reach us?

I said I'll leave. Now. With whatever: travel sack on my shoulder;
guidebook in my pocket; camera in hand. I'll go deep in the soil and
deep in my body to find out who I am. What I give, what I am given,
and still injustice has the greater part

Gold wind of life...

Spotlight a

SCENE ONE: Open-air court in the ancient city of Athens. The accused arrive and proceed among curses and cries of Death! Death!

SCENE TWO: A jail in the same city, beneath the Acropolis, walls half-eaten by dampness. On the ground, a miserly straw mat and in the corner, an earthenware jar of water. On the outside wall, a shadow: the guard.

SCENE THREE: Constantinople. In the harem of the Holy Palace, in candlelight, the Queen throws a pouch of gold coins to the Head Eunuch who bows and looks at her significantly. By the open door, his men at the ready.

SCENE FOUR: Drawing room of a large Monastery. Oblong table, the abbot at its head. Sweaty monks come and go bringing news: a crowd spills into the streets, setting fires, destroying everything.

SCENE FIVE: Nauplio. Greek and Bavarian officers outside the King's quarters converse in low tones. A messenger takes the dispatch and heads toward the steps that lead on high to Palamidi.

SCENE SIX: In front of an old and empty lot in contemporary Athens, a crowd, motley with priests and bishops, gathers to cast a stone, "the stone of anathema."

SCENE SEVEN: Low buildings of EAT/ESA. In the courtyard, drunken soldiers. Braying and lewd posturing. The officer leaving some cell says something to the military doctor. Behind them thuds and cries are heard.

i–vii

I   One day, in the devoted eyes of a young calf, I found again the life I'd lost. I understood I was not born in vain. I started picking through my days, rummaging, searching. I wanted to palpate the matter of emotions. To restore, from the hints I found dispersed throughout this world, an innocence so powerful it washed out blood – injustice – and forced people to my liking.

Difficult – but how else? Sometimes I feel I am so many I get lost. I want to be realized, even along the length of a lifetime exceeding mine.

If even time can't conquer lies, I've lost the game.

II   I inhabited a country emerging from the other, the real one, as dream does from my life's events. I called it Greece as well and drew it on paper to keep it in sight. So slight it seemed; so vulnerable.

Time passed, I kept testing it: with sudden earthquakes, blue-blooded storms. I'd change the place of things to rid them of all value. I studied the Sleepless, the Monastic, to learn the making of brown hills, small Monasteries, fountains. I even laid out a whole garden of citrus fragrant with Heracleitos, Archilochos. The fragrance frightened me, it was so much. So, gradually, I took to binding words like jewels, to cover the country I loved. Lest anyone see the beauty. Or even suspect it isn't there.

III   Roaming my country in this way I found its slightness so natural I said, Impossible, this wooden table with tomatoes and olives by the window must have purpose. So that this sensation, extracted from the wooden square with its few vivid reds and many blacks, can lead directly to iconography. And it, reciprocal, must in a blissful light extend over the sea until the slight's true grandeur is revealed.

I am afraid to speak in arguments belonging by all rights to spring; but only then do I embrace the virginity I profess, and only so imagine her keeping her secret virtue: by rendering useless all the means contrived to maintain and renew her.

IV   I didn't find spring in the fields or, even, in a Botticelli, but in a small red Palm-bearer. Likewise one day, gazing at the head of Zeus, I felt the sea.

When we discover the secret relationships of meanings and traverse them deeply we'll emerge in another sort of clearing that is Poetry. And Poetry is always single as the sky. The question is from where one sees the sky.

I have seen it from midsea.

V   I want to be as truthful as the white shirt on my back; and straight, parallel to the lines of country house and dovecot, which are not straight at all and for this reason stand so certain in God's palm.

With all my pores I lean toward a – how to say? – spinning, awesome *good*. From how I bite into a fruit to how I look out of a window, I feel a whole alphabet take shape, which I try to activate with the intent of joining words or phrases, and the ulterior aspiration, iambs, tetrameters. Which means: to conceive and speak of another, second world that's always first in me. I can even call a host of insignificant things to witness: storm-ridged pebbles, streams with a comfort in their roll, aromatic grasses, bloodhounds of our sanctity. An entire literature inhabits the human soul – ancient Greeks and Latins, the later historians and lyrics; an art, the Well-known, the Full Moon: all can be found in it, transliterated and stenographed by the smooth, the fresh, the rigorous and the ecstatic, and it is their only genuine and authentic reference.

This soul I call innocence. And this chimera my right.

VI   Oh yes, a truly healthy thought – regardless of its reference – endures the open air. And not only that. In our sensitivity it also must be summer.

A little cooler, two or three degrees, it's done: the jasmine shuts up, sky becomes noise.

VII   Smile, bitter lip, my second soul!

I – 7

1   I turned death's face to me like an oversized heliotrope
The cove of Adramytenos appeared with the mistral's curly spread
A bird immobilized between sky, earth and the mountains
Lightly placed one in the other. The child who ignites
Letters now came running to bring back injustice to my chest
My chest where Greece the second of the upper world appears.

These things I say and write so no one else may grasp –
As a plant is content with its poison until the wind
Turns it to fragrance in the earth's four corners –
Will later appear in my bones phosphorescing a blue
The Archangel carries dripping from his arms with huge
Steps fording Greece the second of the upper world.

2   Since falling in love with these small bodies I grew thin, transparent.
Asleep, awake, I thought of nothing else but how to raise them, one
day to bed them. I hid behind doors. Learned to catch them in water,
wind. I still don't know what to call them.

A White or cyanic, depending on the hour and placement of stars.

B Really wet. A pebble.

Γ The lightest; your inability to pronounce it betrays the degree of
      your barbarity.

P Childlike and in fact, almost always, of female gender.

E All wind. The sea breeze takes it.

Y The most Greek letter. An urn.

Σ A pest. But a Greek must occasionally whistle.

3   You're young – I know – and there's nothing.
People, nations, freedoms, nothing.
But *you are*. And while you
Leave by one foot you arrive with the other
Torn by love's light
With or without your will
Piper of plants you come gathering the idols
Against us. Long as your voice lasts.

How when you touch the virgin's cricket
The muscles pulse under your skin
Or how animals who drink then gaze
Erase misery: like you
Take thunder from the Gods
And the world obeys. Go then
Spring depends on you. Accelerate lightning

Grab SHOULD by its D and skin it to its s.

4   I wait for the hour when a
Merciful garden will assimilate
The centuries' outcasts – when a
Girl will declare on her body beautiful
Revolution with trembling voices and pyrotechnic
Fruit returning history
To *go*
      and then
Even the Franks might Hellenize
Arriving at the fig tree's liver
Or taking dictation in their sleep
On the perfection of surf
        and through a mental fissure
The exhalation of some brave
Lavender first met in childhood
Might appease the angry astral space.

5   Three hours' walk outside memory I found myself hunting in the vowel forest. A marksman by instinct (and sentimental) I shoot and bring down:

emblem	May	vial
line	sea	captain
halcyon	oranges	jewel
prey	fountain	dazzling
murmur	tassel	Syrtis
only	gnosis	Marina
mint	metallic	Miletos
rhythm	filter	silver
shrine	deliberate	herald
little	mother-of-god	Monastery
mandarin	pleat	Myrtilla
Pergamos	stellar	blossoming
belt	high noon	languid
sunflowers	fields	March
oracle	morning	cube
mystic	flora	spout

clearing

6   What do you want, what are you after where is the meaning fallen
             from your hands
The music only you hear and the nude
Feet changing earth like a dancer
Who snaps the comet of her hair and a spark
Falls there before you on the rug
Where you see truth betray you

Where do you go, what sorrow, what flaming
Dress rends your flesh, what restored
Ancient fountain meaning to make you oracular
Like this, leaf by leaf, pebble by pebble

Teenager kneeling on the diaphanous seafloor
Whom the more I sleep and dream the more I see
Rising with a basket of seaweed and green shells
Biting the sea like a coin, the same sea who
Gave you brilliance, this light, this meaning you seek.

7   Now that the mind is forbidden and the hours don't
Circulate from garden to garden my thought
Shy as a first-time rosebush
Clinging to the gate
Tries to reconstruct
With darts of brilliant dew
Those age-old greens and golds that in us
Always think it's July seventeenth
So St. Marina's water on the stones again might be
Heard, the fragrant-with-embracing-couple sleep,
The voice
          a voice like Mother's
And barefoot on the Mesolonghi flagstones
Freedom come walk again
As when the poet greeted her – blessed be his hour – in our name
And we've had Easter since.

The Travel Sack

I emptied and refilled my travel sack. "The bare necessities," I said.
And they were plenty for this life – for many more. I started, one by
one, to write them down:

CRETE
Engraved stone seal with representation of chamois
             (*Heraklion Museum*).
The Prince of Lilies (*Knossos*).

THERA
Kore (*Wall painting*).

EGYPT
Portrait of a woman (*Ouserat Grave, no. 51*).
Youth with Antelope (*Menna Grave, no. 69*).

HOMER
dusky water
brightly burnished interiors
then an ineffable ether was cleft from the sky

ARCHILOCHOS
the souls of waves in their embrace

SAPPHO
many-eyed night

HERACLEITOS
extinguish hubris not fire
child's is the kingdom

PINDAR

all equally falsely swim to shore
cold flame
search large Quiet's brilliant light

ETRURIA

Young men restraining horse (*Tarkynia*).
Piper among birds (*Three-bed Grave*).

ATHENS

By Euphronius: Leagros mounted (*Monaco Museum of Ancient Art*).
Team of riders from the Parthenon frieze.
Small Aphrodite statue (*Berlin Museum*).
Aphrodite with flexed legs (*Rhodes Museum*).
Prostitute guarding the grave (*National Archaeological Museum*).
Amynokleia (*Grave stele*).

AESCHYLOS

far-flung wanderings
inky sun-struck race
surf's countless mirth

SOPHOCLES

rains a fresh mist of tears
Sleep, innocent of pain
for you I call eternal sleep

BYZANTIUM

Passage from the "City of Nazaret" (*Kachrieh Mosque*).
Palm-bearer from the Capella Palatina (*Palermo*).
Manuscript by Iakovos Kokkinovafos: Paradise. Its gate and four
        rivers (*Bibliotèque Nationale de Paris*).
Passage from the "Presentation of the Virgin" by Michael
        Damaskenos (*Byzantine Museum, Athens*).
Saint Demetrios. Folk icon of the Macedonian School
        (*Private Collection*).

ANASTASIOS
we all burn in tears

ROMANOS
even my blood black,   where I dip and write
sweetening flower   became a weed to me

DAMASCENOS
in ageless youth
Funereal Mass
O my sweet spring

DANTE
Lo bel pianeta che d'amar conforta
É come giga e arpa, in tempra tesa
di molte corde, fa dolce tintinno

PAOLO UCCELLO
The Battle of San Romano (*National Gallery, London*).

FRA ANGELICO
Left view of the "Coronation of the Virgin" (*Louvre Museum*).

PIERO DELLA FRANCESCA
La Natività (*National Gallery, London*).
Fragment from the "Flagellation" (*Galleria Nazionale delle
      Marche, Urbino*).

EL GRECO
Left view of "Jesus on the Mount of Olive Groves" (*Museum of Art,
      Toledo, Ohio*).

VERMEER
The Atelier (*Federal Museum, Vienna*).
The Music Lesson (*Buckingham Palace*).
The Sleeper (*Metropolitan Museum, New York*).

VIVALDI

Concerto c-dur für Piccolo Blockflöte, Streicher und Cembalo,
    P. 79.
Largo from the Concerto d-moll für Viola d'amore, Streicher und
    basso continuo, P. 266.

BACH

Suite number 2 for flute and strings (1067).
Concerto in F, for oboe, strings and continuo (1053).

HAYDN

Trio in A: H.X.V. number 18.

MOZART

Divertimento in E-flat major for violin, viola and violoncello,
    K. 563.
Allegro from the Concerto for piano and orchestra no. 15 in B-flat
    major, K. 450.
Andante from the Concerto for piano and orchestra no. 21 in
    C major, K. 467.

BLAKE

wash the dusk with silver

BEETHOVEN

Sonata for violin and piano no. 2 in A major, opus 12.
Sonata for violoncello and piano no. 5 in D major, opus 102, 1.

HÖLDERLIN

Ein Räthsel ist Reinentsprungenes. Auch
Der Gesang kaum darf es enthüllen
Denn schwer ist zu tragen
Das Unglück, aber schwerer das Glück

NOVALIS

Sie wissen nicht, dass du es bist der des zarten Mädchens
Busen umschwebt und zum Himmel den Schoss macht
Jahrtausende zogen abwärts in die Ferne, wie Ungewitter

KALVOS

circle-chased sun
and the pelago gets rich
from the smell
    of golden quince

SOLOMOS

for some affairs of the soul
And him in the multi-stellar ether
The turtledove's lament she murmured in her sleep

NERVAL

Mon front est rouge encore du baiser de la Reine

MALLARMÉ

Et j'ai cru voir la fée au chapeau de clarté

PAPADIAMANTES

of the aged oak, who by the cymbal petals of its leafbearing
limbs narrates the centuries' memoirs

Then, through the open window, I saw a star shine
in the interior of the small house

RIMBAUD

Je pisse vers le cieux bruns, très haut et très loin,
Avec l'assentiment des grands héliotropes

KAVAFIS

In the month Aithyr   Leukios went to sleep
a Mrs. Irene Andronikos Assan

YEATS
the moonless midnight of trees

BAUDELAIRE
Nous aurons des lits pleins d'odeurs legères
L'homme y passe à travers des forêts de symboles

MATISSE
Still Life with Oysters (*1940*; *Kunstmuseum, Basel*).
The Plum Branch (*Private Collection*).
Grey and Blue Cutout (*Éditions Verve*).

KLEE
The Goldfish (*1925–26*; *Private Collection, Holland*).
Tracks of Aquatic Plant (*Lyonel Feininger Collection*).

PICASSO
Horse in Circus. Drawing (*The Museum of Modern Art, New York*).
Woman with Fan (*Averell Harriman Collection*).
Woman, Child and Seahorse. Drawing (*Musée d'Antibes*).

BRAQUE
Still Life (*1934*; *Kunstmuseum, Basel*).

JUAN GRIS
Banyul's Bottle (*Herman Rupf Collection, Berne*).
Still Life with Roses (*Private Collection, Paris*).

ARP
Enak's Tears (*1917*; *Private Collection*).
Torso with Flowering Head (*Private Collection*).

ÉLUARD
Une sublime chaleur bleue
D'une écriture d'algues solaires

LORCA
Silencio de cal y mirto

UNGARETTI
Astri Penelopi innumeri

EZRA POUND
you are violets with wind above them

DALI
Nostalgic Echo (*Private Collection*).

ROTHKO
Untitled (*1951*; *Mr. Gifford Phillips Collection, New York*).

THEODORAKIS
The Myrtle
In the Secret Cove
Gloria from the *Axion Esti*

HATZIDAKES
Birds
A Virgin Mary

MOUSTAKI
The Emigré

G. GUSTIN – M. TÉZÉ
Monsieur Cannibale

Spotlight b

SCENE ONE: Bedridden, with a gangrenous leg, Miltiades has been transported to the court and there, with surprise and ultimate despair, hears his condemnation.

SCENE TWO: Patiently, after his ostracism by the Athenians, Aristeides boards the boat that will take him from his land.

SCENE THREE: Pheidias, thrown in jail like a criminal, dies slowly of old age and sorrow.

SCENE FOUR: The forces mobilized by the Thirty plunder and massacre.

SCENE FIVE: After his condemnation, on a pauper's mat, in jail, Socrates, calm, drinks the hemlock and releases his soul.

SCENE SIX: Alexander the Great, standing outside his tent, orders the execution of his devoted General Parmenion.

SCENE SEVEN: In a general melee, Phokion and his friends, not allowed to defend themselves, are sentenced to death.

viii–xiv

VIII   Naked, July, high noon. In a narrow bed, between rough cambric sheets, cheek on my arm I lick and taste its salt.

I look at the whitewash on the wall of my small room. A little higher is the ceiling with the beams. Lower, the trunk where I have set all my belongings: two pairs of pants, four shirts, white underclothes. Next to them, the chair with the huge matting. On the floor, on the white and black tiles, my two sandals. I also have by my side a book.

I was born to have so much. Paradox doesn't interest me. From the least you get anywhere faster. Only it is more difficult. You can get there as well from the girl you love if you know to touch her, and then nature obeys you. And from nature too – if you know to remove her thorn.

IX   "Yesterday I thrust my hand under the sand and held hers. All after-noon then the geraniums looked at me from the courtyards with meaning. The boats, those pulled to land, took on something known, familiar. And at night, late, when I removed her earrings to kiss her as I want to, with my back against the stone church wall, the pelago thundered and the Saints came with candles to give me light."

Doubtlessly a separate, irreplaceable sensation exists for each of us, which if we don't find and isolate in time, and cohabit with later, and fill with visible acts, we're lost.

X   Whatever I was able to acquire in my life by way of acts visible to all, that is, to win my own transparency, I owe to a kind of special courage Poetry gave me: to be wind for the kite and kite for the wind, even when the sky is missing.

I'm not playing with words. I mean the movement you discover being written in an "instant," when you can open it and make it last. When, in fact, Sorrow becomes Grace and Grace Angel; Joy Alone and Sister Joy

with white, long pleats over the void,

a void full of bird dew, basil breeze and a hiss of resonant Paradise.

XI   Fantastic truths perish slower. Rimbaud survived communism as Sappho's moon will survive the moon of Armstrong. Different computations are necessary.

The clock we face doesn't count hours but doles out imperishability and waste, in which we partake either way, as we partake of youth or age. Perhaps for this reason, I was always less afraid of death than illness; a tender body dazzled me more than a tender sentiment.

The sun explodes in us and we stand, palm to mouth, terrified.

The wind is up. The sacred triumphs.

XII   From the pebble to the fig leaf and from the fig leaf to the pomegranate, as from the Kouros to the Charioteer and from the Charioteer to Athena.

I dream an Ethics whose final reduction leads to the same consubstantial and indivisible Triad.

XIII Homer's shores harbored a bliss, a majesty, that reach unaltered to our time. Our feet, gouging the same sand, feel it. We walk, thousands of years, the wind incessantly bows the reeds, and we incessantly raise our faces. To where? Till when? Who governs?

We need a legal code that develops like our skin during our growing years. Something both youthful and strong, like the ancients' *in water everlasting* or *weep blossoming tears*. So what we humans birth might surpass without oppressing us.

XIV I completed my higher mathematics in the School of the sea. Witness some exemplary sums:

1. If you deconstruct Greece, you will in the end see an olive tree, a grapevine, and a boat remain. That is: with as much, you reconstruct her.

2. The multiplication of aromatic grasses by innocence always gives the shape of some Jesus Christ.

3. Happiness is the correct relationship between deeds (forms) and emotions (colors). Our life can be cut, and has a duty to be cut, to the dimensions of Matisse's colored papers.

4. Wherever there are fig trees there is Greece. Wherever the mountain rises above its word there is a poet. Bliss is not subtractable.

5. An evening in the Aegean is composed of joy and sorrow in such equal doses only truth remains in the end.

6. Every progress in the ethical plane must be inversely proportional to the ability of power and numbers to dictate our fate.

7. A "Departed" for half of us is, by necessity, a "Revenant" for the other half.

8–14

8   As in   in a kiss's eon
     I can't catch you Fate
                  I you liv   in shade
        hammer   cheekstone in the veins
                    where points the masthead alw
            birched the sky a peacock
     Rays with white the top clouds   on the hill
     One   Green gold and leafiness of bird that
     Gazes at water through the reeds
                    uninhabited soul from
     Solitary swallow you brought me a tear.
                    now
         mourning
     With fresh arg   cave that just broke
     And ha
                  of old trees
     Dreams incl   as island by waves   and there
     At shore's edge
     Smeared Ethiopianlike with Moon   high
               homeless families of stars and maps
     That angels draw with an invisible right
     Hyp   ra   as always.

9   Have you ever thought of it,
     The grape, at the hour when love shapes you
     As time shapes the stalactite? And the orange, have you
     Seen it stirring in your dreams
     Once Maria – twice young moon
     The foliage all still dark
     And heavy with death too slow to scatter?

What does it mean
To be from a good family as the cricket from a fir ax
How equally meaningless and ready for loss
And ready for duration in golden time are you?

Child – you dare call me! Play if you dare
Pretend me a plant – wrap me a wind
Enter a virgin's sleep and bring her dress
In your teeth like a dog. Or if not, then
Bark, bark, behind your shadow
As I have, a whole life, inside high noon.

10   I speak with the patience of a tree that rises
In front of a window as old as it
Whose shutters are eaten by the wind
Who keeps pushing it open and keeps wetting

With Helen's water and with words
Lost in the dictionaries of Atlantis
One I – and from the other side the Earth
Side of destruction and of death.

The tree that knows me says "hold on"
It gathers clouds and keeps them company
As I keep to white paper and to pen
On nights that have no clock to see

The meaning of "you shouldn't," "it's not right."
I have seen virgins, I have opened
Their downy shell to find the inner
Side of destruction and of death.

11   L U C K H A L F K I L L T H E O T H E R H A L F F O R Y O U
G R E E K S C O M E S A Y O U N G D A U G H T E R W I T H S
U N F L O W E R I N H A N D A S K I N G F O R J U S T I C E
A N D N E V E R S H O W I N G W H I C H M O U N T A I N L I
N E I N H E R O P E N P A L M I S A R O A D W I T H W I N D
I N T H E H A I R A N D V O I C E O F W A T E R S S E A T H
E C A N I S T E R T H A T N O F O R E I G N E R I M A G I N
E S H E L P I N G W I T H F I L L S W I T H H I S T H U N D
E R A L W A Y S A L O N E T H E O N E T R E A T E D U N J U
S T L Y A S T H E S P R I N G U N D E R T H E S T O N E O F
F A T H E R S U N T I L F I N A L L Y O N T H E H O U R Y O
U W I L L S P I L L W I T H F O R C E O C L E A R L I G H T

12   Just for a moment play on your guitar
The names of the Virgin and you'll see

Hey hey Golden-haired
Hey hey Golden-staired

The mountain leap again a white house on its flank
The two-winged horse
And the sea's wild strawberry you'll see

My Luminous my Channel and my By-the-door

The green boat bob and vanish in the cornrow surf
And Mitsos with the hair and little chain around his neck

Hey Lady of the Well
Hey Virgin So Much Water

Curse and raise unsuspecting in his nets
Four or five ancient Greek words
A *téllesthe* and a *neusí*, a *mélea* and *krínai* like

Karystian and Kleidian
Daphnian and Argeian

Just for a moment play them on guitar
And from the burning pelago out front you hear

Hey Crystalline hey Morning Dew
Hey Virgin of the Victors

The scrim of sky being torn in two
And an ancient adolescent identical to you
Descending – look:
Upright atop the waves with a harpoon and on the white
            foam floating

Cave-dweller Myrtle-limbed Sea-going hey!

13   They're always safe in me
     At anyone's disposal: the lunging but immobile
     North boulder
     The solitude of sacred surf
     And the infernal sleep four times
     More powerful with a Zeus all its own thundering
     On an invisible white beach.

     Signs in the air: zeta – eta – omega
     (High at the hour when down deep
     A foaming Sikinos goes by)
     Perpetually transmit that pain
     Rings falsely in the body
     And danger – you need but be a strong
     Helmsman or a Kite
             to quickly pin him.

14   To Beauty, to Mary, the bipolar star
     Who holds a dove and shines her hand.

Aegeodrome

When I opened my guidebook I understood. No maps or anything.
Just words. But words leading precisely to what I searched for. And
slowly, turning the pages, I saw space being shaped like a tear by deep
emotion. And I inside.

agape	bluefish	chicken coop
Alexandra	bluefly	cicada
All Souls' day	blueing	cistern
anchor	boat	citrus
anemone	bolt	Claire
Anna	bougainvillea	clear sailing
ant	boulder	cliffs
arch	braided rug	clockwork
arm in arm	bride	cobblestone
armoire	brine	colored pebbles
aspen	butterfly	comb
astringent		cool wind
August	café	cork
	cage	cove
bait	caïque	crab
barbette	canary	cricket
barrel	candle	crops
basil	candlestick	cross
basket	cape	cuttlefish
bay leaf	captain	cyclamen
beach	cardamom	cypress
beam-reach	cardinal	
beeswax	castle	dandelion
bell	caulking	daphne
bergamot	cemetery	deckhand
birdsong	chameleon	desert island
bitter sea	chamomile	dogwood
blanket	chapel	dolphin

donkey
doublemint
dovecot
dragnet
dry
drystone
dumb

East wind
easy
echo
eggplant
Eléni
embers
eucalyptus
exile

fair
fallen olives
farmer cheese
fern
feta
fiancée
fig
filter
firefly
fireplace
fisherman
fishhook
fishing lights
fishing line
fishing net
fish soup
flag
flashlight
florins

flowerpot
flower water
foam
fortunetelling
fountain
frankincense
frapped
fresh
Froso
frost
funeral walk

garfish
geranium
ghost
girl
glare
goat
gooseberry
grandma
grape
grass
gull
gust

halter
hare
harpoon
hedge
heliotrope
high ceiling
high sea
holy water
honeysuckle
horse of the Virgin
hurricane

hyacinth
hydrangea
hyssop

icon
incense
Indian fig
isthmus
ivy

jar
jasmine
jib
jujube
July
jumping-jacks
June

keel
kerchief
kilns
kiss

lament
lampblack
lapping
latch
lavender
lemon tree
licorice
lighthearted
lighthouse
light-shadowed
lily of the shore
limpet
little bell

little stairs
lizard
lobster
locust
loom
low wall
luff

mad
magic
Mall
mandarin
Mando
marble
Marina
marzipan
mast
mastic
mat
medusa
melon
memorial
mint
mistral
monastery
moon
mooring
morning joy
moss
motorboat
muleteer
mullet
muscat
must
myrrh
Myrtle

naranja
nettles
noon
Northeasterly
North wind

oars
ochre
octopus
offering
oil lamp
oil press
old man
olive
omelet
orange
oregano
Orion
ouzo
oven
ozier

pail
Palm Week
pampas
parapet
pass
pebble
pelago
perch
perpendicular
petal
pew
philodendron
phylactery
pine

pine resin
pinna
pistachio
pitch
pitcher
plane tree
plank
Pleiades
plum
poppy
port
prime
promise
prow
psalter
pumice

quail
quince

radishes
rascal
ravine
red earth
red lead
red mullet
resin
rope
rose
rosebush
rosemary
rowlock
ruins

saddle
sails

St. Anargyri
St. Mamas
St. Monica
St. Paraskevi
salt
salutations
sandstone
schooner
scorpion
sea
seabird
sea breeze
sea cave
seafloor
seal
sea urchin
seaweed
seine
September
sesame
shack
sheepskin
shell
shrimp
shroud
silvered
sirocco
sister
sleep
slip
small bridge
smallfry

source
Sou'westerly
sparrow
spinning wheel
sprite
squall
stalactite
starfish
starlight
stern
stone ship
stone sill
storm
strait
such
sun
swallow
swordfish

tassel
Taxiarch
tent
terraced
three-masted
threshing ground
tiller
tillia
tomato
turpentine
turtledove

unspoken water

vessel
veteran
vine leaves
vines
vineyard
viper
virgin

wash
watermelon
watersquash
wave
weed
well water
Westerly
whitefish
whitewash
wild cherry
wild dove
wild goat
wild pear
wind
windmill
woodbine
woven

yard

zephyr
zucchini

Spotlight c

SCENE ONE: The first Christian King, Constantine, orders his own son, Krispos, arrested and put to death.

SCENE TWO: Heracleitos's men have led his nephew Theodoros and his illegitimate son Adalarichos to the torture chamber. They cut off their noses, hands, and right feet.

SCENE THREE: Having blinded her minor son Constantine, Irene the Athenian proclaims the eunuch Stavrakios, Grand Justice.

SCENE FOUR: Theophano secretly leads her lover Ioannis Tsimiskis to the matrimonial chambers of the Palace so he can murder Nikiforos Phokas.

SCENE FIVE: Inside the church, during the memorial service for Emperor Theodoros Laskaris, Michael Palaiologos murders the minor Ioannis IV and takes his place.

SCENE SIX: During Christmas matins Michael Travlos, aided by six other conspirators, kills his benefactor Emperor Leon v.

SCENE SEVEN: Andronikos Komnenos strangles his nephew Alexios and marries his widow who is thirteen years old.

xv–xxi

xv My childhood years are full of reeds. I spent a lot of wind growing up. But only so did I learn to separate the slightest whispers, to speak precisely among the mysteries.

A language like Greek where *agape* is one thing and *eros* another; desire one thing and longing-with-a-beating-heart another; bitterness one thing and marasmus another; guts one, entrails something else. In clear tones I mean which are – alas – grasped less and less by those who more and more are distanced from the meaning of a celestial body whose light is our assimilated labor, just as it doesn't cease revolving every day, all brilliance, to reward us.

Whether we want to or not, we are the matter as well as the instrument of a perpetual exchange between what sustains us and what we give it to sustain us: the black we give to receive white, the mortal, everlasting.

And we're indebted to some bright duration for our potential joy.

xvi The soul too has its dust, and woe if the wind doesn't stir in us. Urges beat down our windows, glass shatters. Few know the emotional superlative is formed of light, not force. That a caress is needed where a knife is laid. That a dormitory with the secret agreement of bodies follows us everywhere referring us without condescension to the holy.

Ah! when time comes to sit on some St. Prekla's sill among wild figs, red-fruited mulberries, in an abandoned place, a jagged shore, then little Button, candle in her hand, will reach on tiptoe for the flammables inside our sigh: spites, passions, cries of rage, ten thousand confetti insects brightening the place.

XVII   And there, in the midst of misery, from Santorini's excavations, from beyond despair – at last: a Kore Therasia comes proffering her hand as if to say "Greetings O Graced."

I am no painter, Kore Therasia. But I will tell you with whitewash and with sea. Extend you by my writing and my acts. Offer you a life (the life I didn't get) without policemen, without files, or cells. A white bird just above your head.

I'll plant vineyards – words. Build Palaces with what you give me to love. I'll go from Hegeso to St. Ecaterine. I'll bring earth and peace.

XVIII They filled my head since childhood with the image of a death hooded in black, who brings life like a trap and holds it open, baited with bliss. Let me laugh. Who chewed the laurel said otherwise. And it's no accident we all orbit the sun.

The body knows.

XIX   Hi, Beautiful Archangel, blisses like fruit in a pan!

XX   A mountain of wildflowers, wiltless and unchanged as in our thought, trembles each time we manage to turn to air. And to think that, provided we all wanted to, we *can*. As we can span the endless acres of ethics that extend beyond the single and abominable – alas – one, where a most ancient stupidity transfixes us in its almighty endurance.

XXI   I express myself as a bergamot in the morning air. The filtration no one else perceives is what counts. Through social struggle, through the yearning for justice and freedom, through man's inalienables: an aroma!

A person is never as large or small as the meanings he grasps, from the Angel to the Demon. It's like the space left when these two rival forces self-destruct. If it pleases me to refer to a tree's nobility or turn answers to riddles, it's for this: to understudy the child I was and have again on hand, entirely for free, that endless visibility, the mightiest, most enduring of Revolutions.

I was looking at what fit the large square window: some scorched land, a stripe of deep blue surf. Later, in my sleep, three in the afternoon, I saw Hermes descending from the sky, leg flexed, holding a small girl in his arms, head upside down, her hair poured in the wind.

15–21

15   This stone head and broken flowerpots
      Setting like the sun at the hour of irrigation
      In Aegina or Mytilene – this fragrance
      Of jasmine lemon-balm and hyssop
      Keeping the sky at a distance
      If you really are the one
      That moment passing high over the rooftops
      Just like a schooner with open sail

      The girls' songs full of earth
      Where tears shine like Ursa Major
      And the abundant sky-grass you set foot on
      Once, and once and for all exists
      Annexed to your own Greek state
      If you really are the one who lives and lives against
      Superfluous things and days
      The Jesus on the left O
                              then you will understand me.

16   Where shall I speak it, night, in the wind
      Among the loquat stars, in the blackness reeking
      Of sea, where speak the Greek of bitterness
      In capital trees, where write it so
      The wise will know to decipher
      Between the second and third wave
      Such heavy burning mood of stones that didn't sink

      You, St. Salvador, who dress in storms
      Raise the sea's eye and let me travel
      Miles in its green transparence
      To where the masons excavate the sky
      And find again that moment before birth

When violets filled the air and I knew not
That thunder knows nothing of its flash
But strikes you thrice – all light!

17 As in the sky in spring
    Gray-green you appeared
    Winnowing a rain of myriad rays

    And walking toward a slippery slope
    Of stars with a flask of sleep you
    Evaporated having trampled

    The idle-tongued.
    The mountains were veiled by armies
    Of crystalline frankincense

    And not to be outdone night's
    Poppies bloomed until
    Thousand-winged

    Words from your lips
    Restored now wholly
    The once-grasped dreams

    Of mariners.
    Like a goatherd's solitary lantern you
    Lit our soul in the abyss, Kore.

18 Even when they destroy you it will still be beautiful
    The world because of you
                            your heart – true heart
    In place of what they took from us –
    Will still beat and a gratitude
    From the trees you touched will cover us

Unshackled lightning how do they retie you

Now that I have no air no animal companion
Nor even a woodsman's lost thunderbolt
I hear water running
                              maybe from God
(And I blaspheming) or from the mouth
Of a solitary who approached the peak's most Secret Keys
And opened them
                              for this I address You
Night of a Holy Tuesday with the irreplaceable pelago
Facing me – so you can tell it goodbye and thanks.

19   The trotting of good horses will help me
      Say my prayers before sleeping
      On a mat – as I was born – with a little spittle
      Of sun on my forehead and my ancient heart
      Who has all of Homer and so still endures

      Pounding exhaustively in the black stone
      Of Psara a worshipful light
      I bring you future Greek
      Daisies who have put a candied almond in Hell

      I tell with courage of the little gold
      Atop the gates like the birds know
      To leave an idea of joy and then die

      Hi there my faucet open drop by drop
      Again fills azure time

      Who is innocent and has no count.

20   You were saying I should leave yesterday the most
      Lacerated sea we took the candelabrum
      With the thirteen blue myrtle-twigs I am
      Or even if you come a roof with legible below it

      On your body Homer's words
      Surfward reflections
      Airy Poseidon all carnations
      Of signs because fresh I was until.

21   And most important: you will die.
      The other Horn-head will open
      A mouth for you to enter, your face white
      While even the music will continue and on the trees
      Which you never turned to see, the frost will be dismissing
      Your works one by one. So what?
                                    Think now
      Whether truth generates
      Raindrops, whether the galaxy expands
      In fact, then wet, glowing, with your hand
      Atop a noble laurel you'll depart more Greek
      Than I who blew you prime winds in the strait
      Who packed whitewash and tempera in all your luggage
      The little icon with its gold Julys and Augusts
      You knowing all along when I'd be
      Lost, on foot, you'd take me in
      Lifting onto the tablecloth
      The bread the olives and the conscience
      Our first day in the second homeland of the upper world.

The Snapshots

Above all, precision, I would say. And take care to keep the f-stop narrow. When I started developing I saw it clearly: I'd wrested types from moments which, having existed once, nothing ever again could abolish.

A KÉRKYRA

Spring night in a distant country graveyard. That luminous cloud of fireflies that lightly shifts from grave to grave.

MYTILENE

At Mystegna, morning, climbing the olive groves to the chapel of St. Marina. You feel a weight subtracted like sin or remorse, and digested by the coarse soil as if drawn by magnanimous ancestors.

SKIATHOS

Just as the small boat meets the sea cave, and suddenly, from the awesome light, you are enclosed in frozen blue-green mint.

ANDROS

Strapourgies. Moonlight on blossoming ravines all the way to the fragrant unending pelago.

MYKONOS

Small terrace. Between pots of geraniums, a rose dome, white arrows, masts weaving the sky, Delos.

PAROS

"Eletas" farm. Twilight. Ducks and geese. Someone on the threshing floor, asleep, a huge straw hat on his head, his legs half-parted.

KYTHNOS

Spine of the island "Pepper," asymmetrically triangular as twilight approaches from Kanala.

SERIPHOS

Sailing along the island at high noon. Your nude arms burn on the prow. The small embraces keep unfolding, one from the other, until at last the great one opens out, the white crown on its head.

AEGINA

Eleven o'clock, wind on the uphill to Old Chora. Not a soul.

SPETSES

St. Anargyri. The luminous seafloor in the shallows full of little holes, and above the pine, old, broken, unloading its fragrance as if paying back an old debt.

HYDRA

Holy Friday. In the boats, priests and boys with cherubim. The crowd lit with candles. O my sweet spring…

PATMOS

The trembling surf pale, and the conical boulder facing it heavy, dark. The *dook-dook* of an unseen motor schooner passing by is heard.

RHODOS

In the old Greek quarter. Whatever the eye can catch from half-open doors: barefoot babies and huge banana leaves. In the background laundry on the line, a cat.

CYPRUS

In "Sultan Tekeh" just outside Larnaka. Leaf shadows shift rhythmically in the wind and seem a sieve worked ceaselessly just like a conscience.

AIX-EN-PROVENCE

Suddenly spring. Between sculpted railings, a girl's head, looking perplexed.

ST.-JEAN-CAP-FERRAT

The seaside trail leading to Beaulieu. To the left, a huge garden with multiple terraces and a tall dog staring haughtily. To the right the sea, almost white. Smell of fresh cut clover.

PALERMO

Church interior as it appeared in my sleep. Reddish frescoes and, on the floor, black and white tiles. Heat.

AMPURIAS

Autumn afternoon among the ruins. You gaze at the sea, dull in the fine rain, and think about a lost Greek empire. For the sake of language, not anything else.

CÓRDOBA

Diminutive *patio* in a poor neighborhood. Little fountain, arches, openings behind them curtained off with beads. Two shorn boys, full of curiosity, stop their game to observe the stranger.

CONSTANTINOPLE

From the deck of *Felix Dzerdzinsky*. A crowd of fierce faces on the pier. Far in the distance, among the minaret spears, Aghia Sofia.

CAIRO

In the dust and crowd of a common quarter. A funeral procession with Coptic priests whispering incomprehensible words in the blazing noon.

B AEGINA

Blend of Hyssop and Jasmine at midnight.

SPETSES

The prow pitching and beating on the waves. Each time, foamdust, full on the face.

ZAKYNTHOS

Twilight on the Cape, in the old house of Dionysios Solomos. Silence and awe in front of the large, round, stone, garden table. And a simultaneous undercurrent of strange comfort.

MYTILENE

A spoonful of blackberry preserves after afternoon sleep.

CHIOS

Pyrgi. From the unbearable heat to the moist interior of the church. A sensation of whitewash and half-vanished frescoes the length of the body.

SIFNOS

Room with arches. The naked body as native, you might say, as when you were born in the solar ossuary.

KALYMNOS

A red snapper broiled with plenty of choice oil and lemon.

C ANNOULA

As she bathes, having finished the laundry, in the large stone basin of the house. White luminous body.

ALEXANDRA

Who studies for entrance exams while absentmindedly caressing her left breast and then, using the pencil in her hand, rhythmically embroidering its nipple.

SPERANZA

As the moon advances and captures her feet-first. She floats on her back in its light and, from the rise and fall of her nude breasts, a scent of garden and of sea arrive.

DEMETRA

High on the chimney of the roof. The wind takes hair and dress. Her very skin glows and she turns left and right like a bird, inexplicably happy.

BILLIO

Who lets her nightgown drop, picks it up, discards it finally and sits facing the balcony, her bra unfastened in the back.

INO

At night before sleep. She waters the plants in the strong veranda light, her body outlined under the gauzy nightgown. You confuse her with the flowers.

POPPY, ANGELA, HARIKLEIA

Who sleep deeply: one with her thighs this way; the other's hand on a naked breast; the third's right leg flexed, arms high around her head. While a breeze of bruised violet and lemon tree rounds the door's lip.

Spotlight d

SCENE ONE: Odysseas Androutsos commands that the emissaries of Areios Pagos, Noutsos and Panourgias, be arrested and executed.

SCENE TWO: A special committee acting as a court martial condemns George Karaiskakis as "menace and traitor to the land."

SCENE THREE: Condemned to death, Theodoros Kolokotronis is thrown in jail.

SCENE FOUR: Sunday morning, in Nauplion, outside the church, Governor Ioannis Kapodistrias falls to the Mavromichaels' bullets.

SCENE FIVE: Leaving the Gare de Lyons, in Paris, after the signing of the Sèvres pact, Eleutherios Venizelos receives the bullets of two Greek officers.

SCENE SIX: Under German occupation, the Greek Popular Liberation Army exterminates Colonel Psaros, who is fighting for the same exact cause as head of an independent guerrilla group.

SCENE SEVEN: In Cyprus, men sent by the Dictator government of Athens set a trap for National Leader Makarios, who just manages to escape.

xxii–xxviii

XXII   Sometimes I go into the air as if reading the Iliad. I take the path that leads above the houses, high, and, as cove and embrace change their shape with my ascent, emotions too change place and form in me: the identity of heroes, the savage satisfaction of saying *no*, the direct, the luminous, the never twice the same.

A dark teenager whose undergarment has been lowered and who remains beautiful next to all kinds of indigo and black. Hard to see in Christianity; impossible to find in Marxism; small Alexander the Great over the Aegean he embodies and whose light surf never ends.

XXIII   The sun must surely have a childhood as a clear waterdrop. That's why he glimmers in an eyelash; and keeps the coolness on the frescoed Saints, July, high noon.

Not to mention transparency. Which, if luck lets you love a girl, you see within: as in poems.

If it is possible to die without perishing, it must be so: a transparency where your final components – fire, dew – being visible to all, one way or another, you too will exist in perpetua.

XXIV   For whom the sea in the sun is a "landscape" – life seems easy and death as well. But for anyone else it's a reflection of immortality, it is "duration." A duration whose own blinding light prevents you from perceiving.

If it were possible to stand, at the same time, before and after things, you'd see how much time's chasm, which simply devours events, loses its meaning: as in, exactly, a poem. And then – since a poem develops the instantaneous or, conversely, contracts the infinite – one can earn one's freedom without resorting to any kind of explosives.

If we could only understand one thing: that everything isn't held by the living.

xxv   A transliteration of the sound achieved by the *pafflapping* of small surf, while the moon gains distance and the house draws near the shore, could reveal a lot. About the crowns of the senses, for one. Where gentleness, supplanting power, always arrives first: a glowing pistachio-green, the pebble lit, the wind's solitary footsteps on the leaves. Or else: something frontal, a dome, rendering nature linear as the surf's purl turns the Greek tongue ecumenical.

Learn to pronounce reality correctly.

xxvi   Pronounce reality as the sparrow does the dawn. And approach it as a ship does Serifos or Milos. Where mountains unfold one from the other until the splendid cone with its white houses is revealed; one island divided in two or three; and the perpendicular boulder is seen, up close, to hold the most virgin white embrace. Profound penetration into the senses and simultaneously constant reversal of any utilitarian concept about the nature of the material world.

Nowhere did I feel my life so justified as on a ship's bridge. Everything in its proper place: sheet metal, pipes, screws, cables, flotation devices, airshafts; and I myself inscribing the constant transformation by remaining fixed. A full, self-sufficient and organized world that responds to me, and I to it, and together we penetrate miracle and danger as one body.

Enduring ship, my land.

xxvii   I was late in understanding the meaning of humility, and it's the fault of those who taught me to place it at the other end of pride. You must domesticate the idea of existence in you to understand it.

One day when I was feeling abandoned by everything and a great sorrow fell slowly on my soul, walking across the fields without salvation, I pulled a branch of some unknown bush. I broke it and brought it to my upper lip. I understood immediately that man is innocent. I read it in that truth-acerbic scent so vividly, I took to its road with light step and a missionary heart. Until my deepest conscience was that all religions lie.

Yes, Paradise wasn't nostalgia. Nor, much less, a reward. It was right.

XXVIII We walk thousands of years. We call the sky "sky" and the sea "sea." All things will change one day and we too with them, but our nature will irretrievably be carved on the geometry we disdained in Plato. And in it, when we bow, as sometimes we bow over the waters of our island, we'll find the same brown hills, inlets and coves, same wind-mills and the same abandoned chapels, the small houses leaning on each other and the vineyards asleep like children, the dovecots and the domes.

I don't mean these themselves. I mean the soul's same natural and spontaneous movements that generate matter and order it in a specific direction; the same pulses, the same lifting up toward the deeper meaning of a *humble Paradise*, which is our true self, our justice, our freedom, our second and true ethical sun.

Exit

BUT INCONCEIVABLY NO
                one hears. The bird of Paradise
ever flies higher in flames. The voice turns elsewhere,
the eyes stay miracle-free.

      Abandoned are the eyes

One among the thousand murderers, I too take the innocent, the
weak. I wrap the ancient garment round me and descend the stone
steps again, calling and exorcising

      Abandoned are the eyes you call

eons now over the blue volcanoes. Far in the body and far in the soil
I stand on, I went to find out who I am. Rich in small joys and unex-
pected meetings, look at me: incapable of learning what I give, what
I am given, and still injustice has the greater part

      Gold wind of life...

Selections from

Open Papers

… I'd like, in presenting these texts, to confess at once: I am not a critic or a prose writer. Psychological analysis does nothing for me, my powers of observation are largely absent, and every attempt at description bores me to death. I have no way to exhaust a subject except to live it… writing. Which means I dive in a long way before clarifying what I want to say, I let myself drift, here and there, preferring the darkest corners, trying to *see* or, if not, at least to *touch* and *recognize*.

As much as I can. Because, unfortunately, currents often take me, I lose myself near something I like and – as my pen runs away with its own charm, arousing in me other instincts – I notice, as soon as I exit this strange swim, that I have drifted far, sometimes not even having touched what I was after. To be more precise, only then do I know what I must say. But it is already late. You don't step in the same river twice, to honor in my turn the great Ephesian.

~

I know how ultimately difficult simplicity can be and do not need to be referred, again, to the Ancients. Simplicity was different for the Ancients. Their hands had not yet met the wrinkle; that is, they had not yet come across the need to efface it. But as soon as every cheek is no longer fresh, your longing to caress makes you invent a newer, tighter skin.

~

But if you catch birds with woven reeds, you never catch their song. For that you need another kind of reed, a magic reed, and who can manufacture it if not given it from the beginning? Bless its existence! Where it touches words and their marriages, the true night falls and the actual sun rises and all violations lose their simple – as the simple see it – arbitrariness, assuming instead the same position in contemporary texts that orthodoxies once had in the classics. Revirgining is their justification. Or, in other words: the splendor of youth and error.

~

I'm trying to express with today's words the emotion I had then; I found it again only in the spells which I observed, with fear and unrestrained admiration, being cast by our old Cretan cook. There was of course the ritual aspect, the repeated crossings, the drops of oil shaken in water, the sizzling, burning hairs, and the icons sprinkled with basil buds. But above all were the words, strange ("madtrap" mother would call them), entirely unrelated to anything else I heard and incoherent, "a transposition of dream into verbal idiom," as I might define it today. If I might speak of old impressions unintentionally gathered and corrected by later experience, I could assure you that a wave of mystery rose from the material body of the poem and, in it, the heretic use of speech corresponded to the heretic manner of the script. The older I got the more this correspondence deepened and reached the common root where the phenomenon of language and its symbolic representation meet.

↫

As each wave of Poetry, having first crashed against my youth, returns to me, I feel closer to the light. Inside me, the meaning of Resurrection is inseparably bound to the meaning of Death, and very early on, in the secret region that is the antechamber of Birth. I rediscover my utter frugality in my peaceful symbiosis with such an enigma, for instance my intimacy with the coherence of secret meanings or the ritual that adds two angel wings to man; finally, in my fierce, characteristic emotion of pride, I come to find the words that make me an enemy of the grimace in Art (and in Life, of course), and make me obey the secret voice dictating without pause: *That which disempowers you is unfit for your song.*

↫

Full noon, July, my eyes dazzled by the infinite lacerations of sun on surf, so much so that if the olive groves didn't exist I would have invented them in just such a moment, like a cricket. This is how I imagine the world was once created. And if not created better, human fear is at fault and should look at itself and admit what it is before it speaks. I speak. I want to descend, to fall into this blossoming fire and be taken up like an angel of the Lord...

↫

I have conceived my form somewhere between a sea emerging from the whitewashed little wall of a church and a barefoot girl whose garment is lifted by the wind; a lucky moment I strive to capture and trap with Greek words.

Here is the smallest canvas where my life's ideogram can be embroidered; if you think it worth examining, it would be enough to yield a space whose meaning lies not in the natural elements that compose it but in their extensions and correlations inside us to our farthest limits, so that, in order to become easily read and understood, the entire significance of the vision is finally concentrated in the psychic clarity it presupposes and needs. To understand me one must be convinced *a priori* that the psychic work necessary to conceive of an angel is more painful and frightening than that which manages to midwife demons and monsters.

Death is the first truth. The last remains to be known. The sensation of "things turning" is familiar to me, just like the wave of Poetry I mentioned earlier, crashing against my first youth and returning, here where I wait, smaller each time but still standing, as I had wished, unrepentantly in love, arriving at the secret meeting place early, always with the same longing, the same tightening throat, the same pacing up and down, waiting... For what? Perhaps for what thickens and presses on the chest if not allowed to rise and fall as tears, and then the whole world seems suddenly so sweet and bitter. Sometimes it is a girl, sometimes two or three verses, often simply summer itself.

The way a bird leans to one side, or the yogurt vendor calls a little louder on the downhill at dusk, or the way an odor of burnt grass billows through the open window (from where?), the subtlest, most invisible marks assume their entire meaning, as though their only mission was to convince me that at any moment the beloved arrives. *This is why I write. Because Poetry begins where death is robbed of the last word.* It is the end of one life and the beginning of another, the same as the first but deeper, as deep as the soul can scout, at the border of opposites where Sun and Hades touch, the endless turn toward the Natural light which is Logos and the Unbuilt light which is God. This is why I write. Because I am enraptured by obeying whom I don't recognize, who is my whole self, not the partial one wandering the streets and "listed in the draft registers of the *Polis*."

It is correct to give the unknown its due; that's why we must write. Because Poetry unlearns us from the world, such as we find it; the world of decay we come to see as the only path over decay, just as Death is the only path to resurrection. I know I speak as if I had no right, as if I were almost ashamed to love life. It's true, once they forced me even to this. No one knows; no one has ever discovered from where our passionate hatred toward the possibility of our salvation comes. Perhaps we'd rather not know – but do know – that it exists, and that we are the reason we can neither know nor surpass it. Willing or not, *we are all hostages of the joy of which we deprive ourselves*. Here springs love's pre-eternal sadness.

⤺

Coincidence, when raised to a symbol, occurs with mathematical precision at the most crucial moment, even for the squarest of minds. A moment the rest of us call higher will, Fate's gesture, something like that. I suspected it even as a child; it stirred behind my curtains, in street scenes, I watched it with the light anxiety of wondering whether the unknown taps your shoulder for good or ill. I was right. By the third or fourth page of the text I was so bent on writing, I froze: impossible! I flung my pencil, along with all the imaginary gardens, and went to the window.

There, a young girl had hung two ropes from the mulberry of the inner courtyard; she was swinging!

Each forward swing struck me like the raw March wind already hiding the subtle velvet of white petals, each backward swing extracted from my breast the fragment intended for my private Paradise which, by all indications, I'd never find. I was not, never had been, a sentimentalist. I'd never before even imagined I might direct words of worship to those curls. What then? What was it? *Sensation, self-isolated and assigned to an eternal moment.* That's what it was. I see it today. Perfection achieved only as lightning, the briefest duration necessary to negate our daily misery! Beauty is harsh, as they say: there's a cliché not yet worn out. And, confidentially, the only.

⤺

The seizure of childhood is, in the realm of sensitivity, a demonic machine whose unplugging, when the moment tolls, leaves us awe-struck. We are then slowly reduced to disbelieving ourselves for the sake of those unwilling to believe in themselves. Then why write? Why make Poetry? I ask as in: Why make love? From sender to re-ceiver, nothing mediates the cheeks of a girl, the lines of a poem. The translation occurs without interpreter, the gold dust on our fingers seems enough. And if the wind should blow again? Then all of nature will be inhabited by a million secret signs, and the demon of the in-satiable lying in wait inside us will open its maw for more and more.

⤳

Stone, plant, girl: if their existence extends beyond their surface calm or agitation, then Poetry, and art in general, falsely create the im-pression that they add to, transform, or surpass life, while all they do is reveal a part of its deeper essence or render its wondrous function by an instinctual mimetics. Stone, plant, girl: one girl or many – let's be straight, I don't mean the trendy beauty to which they might aspire and might be flattered to possess, but the unknown beauty that trans-forms them into instruments of an orchestra of global music, makes them the juncture of contradictory charms, transfigures them into the locus of the human occasion to express its tenderness, its compassion for the smallest thing, as well as its terrible harshness, its implacable advancing, always young and strong, assimilating death in its blood.

⤳

Long before I was aware of the ideal of a Poetry that could record the smallest transformative idiosyncrasies of emotion, I was proud of the generous human freedom that believes not only the *extant* but also the *possibly extant*, and so passes into a dimension of divine the-ory where *eros, a simple tree in a storm,* or *a song* are now equivalent.

⤳

Here, now as then, exhausted perhaps by our peregrinations, we need a little silence before hearing again with a virgin ear the huge, susurrating poplar of our thoughts.

~

Even when an idea seduces us without sufficient reason and threatens to expose us to serious accusation we must never, I believe, abandon it. The fact that we lack the arguments to defend ourselves is insignificant next to our obligation to track the mysterious attraction that we may one day discover was not accidental. Not to mention that no one has decreed that we must defend ourselves, for anything. It's time to reclaim this part of our writer's flesh from servitude – to let the sun see it.

~

My insistence on achieving the largest possible transparence in all I undertake originates in the understandable longing to read my thoughts deep in the thoughts of others. Alas, it rarely occurs. More likely I offer a glass of water and hear, "What great liqueur – where did you find it?" Meanings not even *in* my vocabulary... optimism, say, or joy (except if it's the other joy) or the picturesque (what's that?)... occur again and again to my critics. "Clear view" becomes carefree; "penetrating natural *being*" becomes sightseeing; "innocence," well-being. It's all so easy. If they only suspected what bitter roots must stir, what darkness must be counterbalanced, for innocence to endure our days... Bah! We understand coffins, we already gaze protectively at our immature interlocutor, as if only we possess the secret that humans die. "But that's just why," the poor one whispers, but the daily papers are due any minute with their screaming headlines. Who has the time?

~

The true poet scorns overstatement, illustration, and documentation. He makes the invisible visible, the noetic sensate, and the irreal real. He replaces a poor strand of words with one more suited to inspiring unknown visions than to recalling the known. The typical simile, based on analogy and "like" (this is like that), annoyingly reminds him that someone is speaking and underscores a collusion between poet and listener by which the latter undertakes to believe whatever the former fancies to tell him. By contrast, in contemporary poems the world explodes triumphantly and is whatever it wants, each time, to be. Analogy yields to *identification*. This is that. Surprise, small or large, leaves no time to consider whether something is possible or not; it does not brook debate; what the poet says *occurs*.

〜

Panayi, Panayi, I call you back to active duty, and let the cops be suspicious! Didn't you stay with me while others slept, midafternoons? Didn't we eat melon seeds awaiting the ship to round the cove of Hermione? Didn't you pretend to chase me so we could run through my cousin's legs as she ironed in her short pink slip, bare-armed, her hair wet? It's not what you think; that's not what I want from you; I want the first glimpse of the world. May I never lose Columbus's emotion. There are so many little things no one has managed to explore.

〜

Life, life, how strange, how beautiful you are! Surely one day the war will stop. Surely a tree crazy with birds will always exist; so will a girl in love, swearing wholeheartedly – what miracle – on her love. Where could Poetry swear but on this oath: the ultimate oath that raises life to the dignity of emotional self-determination, that raises action to the free function of thought, and eros to the infinite ethics of touching bodies? It is the sun that will preserve the flame of youth's mythos…

〜

Whether you have written poems or not is less important than whether you have suffered, been impassioned or longed for what leads, by hook or by crook, to Poetry. The wind of life hits you before its material body, as the aroma of a woman before her actual presence. What remains is the embrace, and love.

〜

A ceaseless penetration of sea into mountain that was also mountain penetrating sea, the luminosity of water when seafloor is also ceiling over our heads, the bamboo aroma both clearing the sky and erasing our mistakes, the stone fountain on the public road a small daily Parthenon…! Is all that, I ask, a *landscape*? Or merely *nature*? This ultimate reduction drawn so as to be indelible, an order at last whose number is as real and inconceivable as water leaping and shouting like an infant or the moon, coconspirator of breezes, the embrace in which only a lover's vow remains, these palmfuls of wet pebbles I can smell as though my eyes are cleansed by most immaculate meaning… All these, I ask and ask, are *landscape, nature*? Or maybe not. Maybe they are the world's end and beginning, the human alpha and omega, God himself – just as I started to plead Lord have mercy!

No, no, Poetry is a mechanism that demechanizes humans and their relationship to things. The poet beds his contradiction. Linguistically, the temptation to test one's endurance for abnegation often leads to another kind of admission: *this* is a human; what poet dare define him? The truth remains to be invented. Meanwhile, let's speak of simpler things.

↬

"So plausible the Incomprehensible!" I could explain nothing then, nor can I today. Yet I couldn't wait until the house was empty so I could take these verses one by one and let them live in my oral cavity, and not because they were musical. What then? I don't know, a different engulfment, a loss of habit of the tongue and lips (which were losing the habit of the entire world), an oversaturation of syntax to the benefit of the instantaneous soul, brevity at the service of dream… And above all, revirgining. New vocalizations mobilized; blood circulated more; cheeks glowed. I recognized the thrill of young organisms, which, by an irony of fate, I had vainly sought in the innovative but aged Alexandrian.

↬

It's strange, what happens to people! They find it difficult, impossible even, to believe that what they imagine is the same as what they see. They find it difficult to accept that physical phenomena are also spiritual phenomena. They prefer to endure their misery twice – once for their sake, once again for their art's – rather than transform it into a different reality, kneading one potential duration from two sure decays. Primitive people, poets before poems, not having mirrors, literally and metaphorically, in which to preen, overcame evil by reciting terrible, incomprehensible words, just as our island nannies chased demons from our cradles by pronouncing meaningless words with utter seriousness, holding the leaf of a humble weed that assumed, by the very innocence of its nature, who knows what unknown powers. This little basil leaf surrounded by the unknown powers of innocence, the strange words, *is* Poetry, precisely.

ᔔ

If there really is a message sent to us secretly by the part of life we know nothing of, it has never appeared to me as a prowling midnight specter. I saw it, I felt it I mean, at moments when no hand could have yanked the trickster's sheet to expose deceit. The first time was in Olympia: high noon, midspring, chamomile and poppy claiming the holy ground and its fallen marble. No soul in sight, foreign or Greek. Only I, lost by the river, near a rectangular site defined by the foundations of a temple I didn't recognize, being disinclined to archaeology. Heartened, enraptured, I should say, by the total quiet, a little lizard left her hiding place and ran toward the center. At my slightest motion she would stop and wait, full of suspicion, for some seconds, and only when I managed to hold even my breath did she slither, with inconceivable speed, to the symmetrical square stone set higher than the others at the temple's center, as if it were an altar, where the only quiver of sunrays fell through the dense foliage above us, as by a momentary coincidence. I lost sight of her briefly, then saw her climb it and begin to raise her face and stretch her breast to the sun: a sequence of unbelievably small gestures, a balletic system of endless shivers, a palindromic rhythm of barely visible turns, joy and awe became one as in a prayer that touches its destination! I understood that invisible threads were tightening inside me. I felt balanced on a moment of a different duration. God present, as we would say, and who gets it, gets it.

The second time, I was in Spetses. Only my window overlooked the "small back terrace," as we called it. High noon. A small sound drew me to look between the slats of the shutter. Young Irene, the girl of the house, was coming up from the beach, drying herself with a large, bright towel. Drops of sea fell from her hair to her brow, iridesced for a moment in her lashes and, finally, rolled down her cheeks. She found a corner in the sun and in one quick movement spread her towel on the flagstone and lay back, legs half open. Soon, she rose to her elbow, turned her head to make sure no one could see, paused for some time at my closed shutter (inside I held my breath) and then, reassured, loosened her top and lay back down, her disproportionately large white breasts to the sun. A miracle! I faced the crown of a large lemon tree. Below, the low whitewashed wall of the terrace. Next to it, the nude body pulsing in an apotheosis of light. And all in a sonorous background of plashing waves and the cicadas' ji-ji-ji rising invisible, almighty from the garden, the other gardens, the neighboring olive grove, the entire island. I thought I could stand there for hours, an angel in a bizarre photosynthesis.

Just then a brilliantly colored butterfly arrived, drawing large contours in the air. Its wing almost touched my window, I remember seeing its symmetrical black circles. Then without hesitation and in one swoop, it alighted on the young woman's hair. In two leaps it reached one of the beautiful breasts now rising and falling in sleep's rhythm. In the infinitesimal duration of its landing – before it soared off never to be seen again, a butterfly like all the others, soon not to exist, as I would not, nor young Irene – I felt again the sensation of immortality that the parts of life we either hide or allow to be hidden from us can synthesize and provide: the other kind of writing, the second and third Greek, which, when I can read them, cause me to totally distrust all past and present Ecclesiastes.

The miracle returned only once more, in summer, midday, mid-pelago, July, aboard a small vessel sailing form Paros to Naxos. Shouts of "Dolphins! Dolphins!" rang out from the crew, and I saw the gold flashes and arcs in light, like the sheerest net cast and raised, cast and raised, in rhythm, one, two, three, four, until the shapes enlarged, clarified and leapt from the water scattering a myriad drops, a fringe of foam around them, then finally their pointed heads diving straight down at our side, tails broad for a moment in the air, embroidering the blue, a ceaseless embroidery until the needle and the pelagic tablecloth both vanished, leaving the soul alone in the victorious procession

– weightless, unwrinkled, the soul free in the light, the sharp inter-
minable brilliance.

⌒

Beyond this, we can say that the sun's position in the ethical world is
the same as in the natural one. The poet is an intersection of the eth-
ical and natural worlds. The portion of darkness neutralized in the
poet by conscience can be measured in light, a light that returns again,
constantly clarifying the image, the human image. If a humanistic
view of art's mission exists, only so can it be understood: as an invis-
ible function identical to the mechanism we call Justice, and not, of
course, the Justice of the courts, but the one formed equally slowly
and painfully in the teachings of humanity's great mentors, in political
struggles for social liberation, and in the highest poetic achievements.
From such large effort, drops of light fall in the soul's large night,
slowly, like drops of lemon on polluted water.

⌒

Picasso rid me of these complexes by his example. He was almost
an ancient Greek next to me. Half-naked, robust, and blackened by
sun, he lived, in defiance of his millions, in a small humble house in
Vallauris, remarkably like our own island houses. Wearing only a pair
of pants, he painted, went swimming down in Golfe Juan, ate with
enormous gusto, and on all fours played the little horse for Paloma,
his little girl. He enacted the very sensation the Greeks had disowned
– eros and sun in their first, primordial essence – like an ancient
mythic king whose majesty abides not in law and might, but in simple
and comfortable gestures.

⌒

*The poet must be generous. Trying not to lose even a moment of your sup-
posed talent is like trying not to lose a cent of the interest on the small
principal given you.* Poetry is not a bank. It is the antithesis, precisely.
If a written text can be shared, so much the better. If not, it's all right.
What must be practiced – assiduously, infinitely and without the
slightest pause – is antiservitude, noncompliance, and independence.
Poetry is the other face of Pride.

~

This is how the most disobedient child of our era forced the concrete to obey him completely. In direct proportion to his disobedience, he offers us a new notion of the Real and so becomes the first Realist of modern time.

~

The land of Innocence is as borderless and as unexplored as the land of Evil. They are superimposed, or better yet *intra*posed, inside us at the exact point where expedience stops and the concept of commerce becomes useless to the human soul; so they must, of necessity, at some ultimate frontier, share a border. If we had soul-topographers – we do not trust the poets – they could prove just as well, and by linear symbols, that the cost of turning something black to white is *the same* as white to black and always to our spiritual "deficit."

~

FEDERICO GARCÍA LORCA

No one teases the cunning powers of this world with impunity. The shadow of an angel's wing will always mark the gaze of the lost who flirt with the abyss. There comes a day when everything – night, blood, moon, fate, earth's secret cries, eros, a pure human heart, the infinite charm of matter that the wise sought to betray (by the least seductive chimera) and to erect pure beauty's abstract form somewhere else (the Void, of course) – everything returns so simply to the lips of a dark Andalusian galloping *bronce y sueño* through the moon-bathed olive groves of his country. And then, the earth's identity amazingly resembles a masculine song disappearing behind distant mountains. In the name of thirsty grasses, in the name of those who paid in blood for every handful of a newly conquered freedom, drop by drop, Poetry rises to spotlight a fragment of "the eternal holy cross."

~

How beautiful are the Valencian fields when spring, like an infant, opens its eyes and the hours play the sun on their mandolin with a citrus leaf! Life, sweet life, carries no grudge. Beautiful women, erotic women, dancing in colorful skirts as their eyes circle the earth before finally nailing their destination, raise a cloud of dust and swallows in the village square. Thick-shod farmers traverse the fields with their spades. The scarecrows, crooked above the fences, exorcise the carefree sky. Cursing and yelling, sweaty young men drive the bulls to their pens. Saturday afternoon. Old mothers lean from their windows, a secret anguish in their eyes, while in the upper neighborhoods barefoot boys raise hell throwing stones. Why do they drop everything, leap over fences and pour into the fields? What do they know?

꙳

Still, if you're born for the sky you'll find your way to it, even when the natural prototype of the imagined sky turns in your hands to a dry material that you can cut or puncture. Because then you make a fort with it, to crouch in and protect the little morsel that your childhood sense preserved, which now your concentration and prayer will broaden and restore to its initial dimensions.

꙳

Some moments in human life reveal, by a quick imperceptible blink, the surrounding world bathed in strange light, stripped of daily meaning, and recognized by another and first-seen – the real one perhaps? – physiognomy. These are moments when the events that dryly and relentlessly define your way break their orbit, gleaming with different meaning and different goals, moments you suddenly see yourself on never-chosen trails, under strange arches of trees, among people who assume the stature of your most obvious emotions to become *friends*, your friends, as you had always wished them to exist and await you, there, in some bitter corner of your life. No alien element or supersensory presence explains the world's bizarre turn in such moments. Simple, earthly, human, they are the actions and events that occur in a *second circumstance*, more real than the first, one we would distinguish by the name hyper-real.

꙳

Alone at the borders of panic and enchantment, the poet, struck by such fleeting revelation, suffers the passion of adapting his breath to the newly revealed climate; he bleeds to express this secret taste, the indefinable essence, the immortal hue the elements of his internal world swiftly assume. Differently valuating life from that moment on, he painfully measures the distance between himself and the great human plurality. He sees this plurality, entrenched in convention and denying what might cause it to face its essential problems with such frenzied despair, that he comes to understand it is his destiny to undertake, along with the burden of expression, yet another: the burden of empathy, if not the fate of solitude. It is always so: the poet risks, while the misled behind him insist on keeping sealed a door whose lock has long since lost its purpose. Still, though this vendetta between conservatism and change, between natural and unnatural animate development, has remained unextinguished since Heracleitos, we must recognize that it flared with the full weight of its meaning for the first time in our century, insisting that our artists place beauty's eternal element upon the *forever transforming* point of human flow, insisting, in other words, that they feel this truth as the eternal law of their being.

↵

Art-Luck-Risk, yes! *Art*: since for better or worse we long to free the Pythian spark impatient to be Logos, and lead a new evaluation of the world; *Luck*: which unifies colors and shapes, fragrances and sounds, our heart and the heart of the universe in the lyric we dream of; and *Risk*: since, in this society, every true step is destined to a trail of blood, smoke, and tears.

↵

Could ideal communication – the briefest route between two people, a communication felt wholly, like warmth or cold, ravishingly, like eros or terror, mysteriously, like roar of forest or sea – could it become one day the very instrument and goal of Lyric poetry?

↵

Art-Luck-Risk: these three, no other words but these celebrated three (but are they words?) adorned the pages of a year, if not the unveiling of a youth, with chlorophyll's deep-green ink, Eros's deep red and sea's blue deep. Its only philosophy was to elevate truth to the simple and profound stir of live organisms.

⮌

In poetry's countryside the houses no longer have roofs! They are un-covered, and the cicadas wedged in earth's hair sing erotic songs, as do wild birds roosting in the pale-blue wrinkles of deserted bays. There, a couple passes at such hours, embracing always. Eros – let us worship – engenders life through all its surfaces and depths, while heart's hands point to brilliant noon… Oh to walk by a companion's side, voicing emotions… to reunite with elements that cause us once and for all to live!

Selection from

The Outrock Elegies

July's Word

Measured is our space as humans
And to the birds the same is given but
Boundless!
          Boundless the garden where barely torn
From death (before in masquerade it touches me again)
I played and all reached easy to my palm

The seahorse! The bursting bubble's chirp!
The berry's little boat inside deep foliage currents!
And the prow's mast all flags!

Why now they come? Just yesterday I existed
And then the long long life unknown of unknowns
Granted. Just saying it beautifully you're spent; like water-flow
Which soul by soul ties distance
And from one galaxy you tightrope to the next
While underneath your feet chasms bellow. You either arrive or not

Ah lightly sketched upon my sheets, first urges. Fe-
                male angels
Who signaled from above to fearlessly advance in all
Since even falling from the window, the sea
Again will be my horse
The giant watermelon I dwelt in once so ignorant
And the little helpmates, hair unbound
And knowing with wind's intelligence to unfurl over chimneys!
Such joinery of yellow onto blue it truly stuns you
And birdscripts the wind slips across the window while you
Sleep and observe the future

The sun knows. It comes inside you to see. Because the outside
Is mirrors. Inside the body nature lives and from it
                it avenges
As in a holy savageness like Leo's or the Leaver's

Your own flower sprouts
                    called Thought
(Regardless if, though studying, I came out where the swim
From the beginning took me)

Measured is the space had by the wise
And children get the same but
Boundless!
                    Boundless is death, no months or eons
No way to come of age; so to the same
Halls, same gardens you'll return
Holding the cicada Zeus who takes
From galaxy to galaxy his summers.

The Garden with the
Self-Deceptions

I'll begin with a resonance that reaches from the hardest metal to the finest musical string, without excluding pleasures or imposing guilts, but with nature remaining nature.

A way exists to come and go between the daily, so that our clothes remain unsnagged by the spreading branches of self-interest – its insistent stationary march upon our temperament, its subtraction of the tiniest joy that we guard in the safest treasure troves of our private life.

And yet. How different the month of May if, instead of paying tolls to breathe its oxygen, we voiced stone and voiced water, hoping one day to reveal a new grove, appropriate to receive our burial.

Spring is needed, and a life of replete cleanliness, for a gift no one else can give you.

As the Oyster So Its Pearl

I am of the little and the precise. I was never of the third person. I am nourished by the *dys* and the *eu* which I happen to proffer. But I refuse food to the sated who always ask for more, more hunger. It would be like trying to possess my very belongings. Other than that, I can be found where every haze, even the smoke from my cigarette, is neutralized by the little sea Our Lady of Constant Joy keeps for me in her northwest cupboard just in case.

Still, grace is not always a relative who happens to love you. And much time passes before the channels of your mind flood over, and their daimon wreckage dries and goes to wind. Simply: like sleep takes a boy on the hay. And, with his third ear, secretly encodes the pulses of another earth, more his. How beautifully then your hand runs on a low wall of raised words that catch the wild vine of your speech. Everything is about imagination's marrow. How? Malia bay's unstruck water is also father Pindar's quarried stone. Such moments are as if not you but your country's elements, the named earth, speak. And who imagines, imagines.

> Because the Sea
> Stone's manner of pretending
> Storm is shapely
> And the Sirenian consents
> To seahorse fragments stirring on the clay
> Or red earth of some new
> Icarian pelago
> With many droplets' wild-
> Flowers and daisies so that each

Is a life. And the serpentine lines of Knossos urns, the ribs of Ionian pillars, converge:

Where the diamond shows its nail, where night's leaping muslin turns the sky this way. A smart reversal that allows you to intensify the fleet and the enduring at will. And there! As much from distilled citrus and northern lights, Vermion turns more Vermion, as greener from aqua and yellow-gold turns the green of a Naxos ridge, surfing with grass and shells. The sea too has its uphills.

In Greece the mountains, at least to a point, are part of the sea as winters are part of summer. On a different scale, one could say the same for the festive atmosphere, which is part melancholy; more so for revolutionary art which, if of high quality, becomes the starter dough of future law. Here, at this point, one can easily discern how the substance of material and spiritual phenomena is, always and without exception, dual. As each part of matter partakes of another, even its opposite, or as a thought partakes of the more general system of ideas around it, so these two partake of each other, in turn. Let's not be cowed by the agent of chance, through which even a green bean might tangle with quantum theory. It depends on us, our personal manipulation. Because you have two ways of facing chance: accept it as is, as the wind blows it, and give it a stable, immutable place in the geometric sum of your beliefs about existence; or, let it alter your fate and transform you, with its schizoid displacements, into an expressionist copy of your form.

O if I could erase and write people as I want them…

What speech! Here, the retarded monkey in me tries to combine intelligence and void, stupidity and the improbable. How does a thief of good itself operate? Is loveliness hereditary? How many times forty is forty? Does an unloaded conscience peel off and rise to the surface?

Whoever answers must be his fate's only child. Meanwhile the rest of us, tangled with chromosomes, had better desist and throw our impatient kitten its toy. One, two, three times. Only when chance and game return might a small joy of words, if nothing else, be created. Just as from your own vine and hops your sparkling brew is made. And, naturally, on the condition that foul play never intrude. It would be ludicrous to auction off your only good chance, just to rig the prices for your own profit. A penny makes you rich, the many never. From the beginning of this world, an uneven, so to speak, isometry has reigned. The same force is required for both good and evil, since poison acts negatively, as good acts positively, on others, who know how to hold the mirror of clean perception correctly in relations with third parties. Still, the length of what is destined varies. God, so many things, amounting to a little match – strike it on them, and there!

A single flash is man, and who sees, sees.

So many things – not the necessities, of course, may they never be needed, but sensation's pets, which each of us keeps in a warm corner of our heart and for good reason: for that uniqueness each of them contributes to the physiognomy of the common country.

Honor to the olive, for its conscious wisdom.
To louisa, for its noble descent and subtle manners.
To marble, for the one absolute it represents.
To the pine grove, for its tactile and otherwise presence.
To the bitter orange, for ten centuries later it managed
to compress the thought of Ionians.
To the sea boulder, for the memory of the Fathers of All.
To the simply azure, for infinity's similar.

If Not One Were

At the beginning of what the others think of as the end, is heard – for the first time and with all its c's and g's – the music that knows how to shape an eternally repeated embroidery to grace the small fortune of our eyes.

It seems difficult but is simple. You throw the cards and turn them. A plethora of mauve *no*es and red *yes*es appears, silent *always*es, sonorous *never*s, all of them well-placed in geometric designs directly from your soul… Strange. What makes us play a different role in each act of the same play? Why do we mean to be tried over and over?

We exchange futures as lighthouses do their beams, so that, in a final refraction, all our ages resound their "present" at once, just as all our elements – liquid and solid, volatile and crystalline, dark and highly luminous – add up to *one. If not one were passes to another.* So one arrives, encircling every lifeform in the same result as that of the pedestrian and the flyer, relative to the different speed of bodies – although the 1920s futurists had overlooked the fact that everything does flee, but always in one place, like the stars.

ONE MINUTE'S INTERMISSION

The senses too have their chemistry, like those more-than-ten caressing fingers with skins of two qualities, or the preparation, with sharp verbena water, of cyan from ultramarine; finally, LAST BUT NOT LEAST, the traditional opposites, lemon and sugar, as we find them for centuries peacefully cohabiting the depths of a cup of hot tea.

O love, how you depart from eros! You let it reach its utter explosion and exhaust, while you preserve yourself and rise like oil above water to keep the flame of an endless day.

Each day we live, we become unwilling millionaires of image-shards our inner insignificant begets. Who never happened to see the speed and grace with which, night and day, a mother of young birds rises, descends, and gathers from the ground infinite things – tiny seeds, pebbles, leaves, pine needles, straw, and down – to house her babies; who never woke one morning to find a nest under the terrace eaves and thrill to this swift message of life and magic joinery, will never understand that with similarly negligible matter – scraps of illustrated magazines, sometimes also of books – one can achieve, by an analogous magic joinery, the art of the co-image; and so, by analogy, render the vision of a world where graphic sign replaces simple cipher, and transmit a different order of poetic messages, regardless if writing always wins in the last competition.

There were periods we savored as the mad do their freedom. My desk – of the obscure geometry – was practically transformed to a consulate of *idées fixes* and overblown schemas. Daughters of Saint North with glassy epaulets and others with gold disks and an ordained place in the otherwise summery calendar of festivities; boats, prostrate in the scrub oak or barely jutting from their lair, portions of sea as no one has yet seen them, wave-like foals, channels of precious foam. I speak of something that both is and is not. The timely and singular you find on a girl's first page, which vanishes before you explain it.

So worn are we by society and social lies that even the essential truth, directly expressed, seems a paradox.

For the duration of a cigarette, which is our life and where we savor (and self-destruct as also in love) our creative efforts, and anywhere else as well, the only light still shining, though trodden heavily by time, is beauty. That infinitesimal wink in which we tasted beauty and incarnated it once and for all in our private eternity.

As If by Chance

Surprise never looks in the mirror. And sea storm is worn on top, without underwear. It sometimes happens that abstract meanings are rendered by a nimbler tongue than the concrete, which often start to say one thing and say another. Even a photographer, developing, finds things he never imagined. And this is of greater interest.

1. An enormous translucent purple drop, which surely served as hatpin to a nineteenth-century woman.
2. A café, which proportionately fulfills the preconditions of a whole and synthetic poetic work.
3. A goddess – Kore, barely sketched within an otherwise abstract tempera and whom I vainly try, a life long, to render in my way.
4. Guitar solo at night, at the borders of bliss and tears.

Intending to reveal their associative origin, I nail down by chance some of the meanings that, unprepared for, arrive and stick like burrs on pants after a stroll down a dirt path:

1. Fiesole. Open-air antiquarian market.
2. Café Rivoire, Piazza della Signoria, Florence.
3. Glass storefront of small gallery, Rue des Granges, Geneva.
4. Small plaza in the Santa Cruz neighborhood, Seville.

Each art has its secrets which, like humans, also come of age some time. Often their path is slow, like delivery trucks without a map that reach their destination so bedraggled, the addressee does not receive the meaning of their missive. By one character the word eludes you. Order is needed; and order doesn't simply mean, line up a dozen glasses. It means, on another scale, mimic the joinery of molecules of matter till you achieve transparent crystal or a work of art, which is the same.

We're close to where two utter opposites caress: the wildest sensation of expressive freedom coexists with the strictest sense of order, fully apart from form. The distance between the paper you crumple and the one you smooth is at once negligible and immense: the distance, so to speak, between the most terrifying microbe and lottery's winning number. Note that the element of chance is neither excluded nor imposed. It exists outside and independently of the tenets of the game.

Where you sit, a purple drop floats over your eyes. David regards you. Your fingers move upon a square of polychromatic texture. A very young goddess tries to open your iconostasis and emerge. Is a guitar of Andalusian rhythms heard in the distance or maybe the next room?

Surely the force required for the preexistence of opposites is required to conceive the analogies. Regardless of how distant the tenets of the simile might seem. We neither write as we eat nor eat as we write. Yet we drink poetry each time we sip some waking sleep.

A well-written synthetic work of poetry is not so different from a well-laid table. The same rectangular form, the surfaces gleaming like silver, the same moments of self-consciousness trembling in the glasses. A circumstance that makes you want to eat the very paper on which you write and be immediately transformed into a glutton of letters. In other words, to suffer the damnation of the average. What you detest, exactly.

Where the average flowers I cease to exist. I cannot flourish in the mass of each majority. The beautiful minorities are something else. I either make them emeralds to light my night, or eat them with chocolate and cream. That's why no oligarchy I respect comes to power. I choose it precisely for this. So I may never come to power. I come not once but a hundred times to any *Verve*, to *La terre est bleue comme une orange*, to the Virgin of Sikinos before she existed, to *Eau de Vervene*, to *Poem in October*, to Patek Philippe's Nautilus, to Small Green Sea. Precise minorities, rare books, especially if their paper is *Velen pure fil Lafuma* or sixteenth-century papyrus, as found in the antique shops of small European towns.

O Córdoba, with your balconies and towers, Venezia of bridges and *palazzi*, o you Lausannes of conferences and Canterburies of universities, Avignon of Popes, Cannes of casinos. Small towns that over time became the yeast of our future Europe who nursed on the nipple of Greek letters and grew and came of age there, though just when it must remember it, it wishes to forget. It's true anathema to love someone you hate because there's no one else to love.

> *I love all waste*
> *and solitary places, where we taste*
> *the pleasure of believing what we see*
> *is boundless, as we wish souls to be.*

In the School of Winds

It's wind, you can't catch it. Fine. But how does it catch itself? By lifting the corner of the sea's sheet, so high sometimes the sky's nude back is seen, covered with foam and shells? By snagging courtyards and skylights of old houses, roosting and moaning there all night, exploding at first light, furling a line of pure white crests in Mykonos, Ios, Paros? Or by the broken shutter-doors, where in its wrath it starts to speak in ancient carpentries? Yet it can speak pure-blooded Greek if calm prevails: you have but to recite Belthander's and Chrysanza's passions to see a lively, small, and mistral-leavened sea spread all around.

How lovely to caress the hand caressing you and hold its wind and give it to the future like an old flower-vendor proffering from your basket jasmine earloops, gardenia rings, ephemeral, eternal. Wind, wind, Tenos's only son, Cyclades' fecund parent, who signs your name in girls' loose hair and drums on splashing prows, treat us to wisdom taught by Hera's son, so that neither danger turn antagonist to sail, nor sail antagonist to danger.

Hera's young son, are you also sweet Aphrodite's? Do sea peaches flourish also in your breast? Invisible benefactor of colors, sibilation's thief, sublime sound's expert is what you are. With you we see like hearing and hear like seeing a Poseidonian blue or Mycenean gold, not to leave out the Arignotic iodines or gusty Adramytenos's unexpected vineyards. Thankfully hungry ears increase sound, transforming it to color, and it again translates multiple hues, coequal meanings able to turn to icons and so on. Which means we always walk a bit ahead, a bit behind our senses.

> Grown sevenfold the ears are unquenched
> By pelago
> The seven moist greens
> The dark close and untouchable
> A bit more open
> My bitterness my unlike-any-other's more open

A chill cry like a future
The secret fruit-tree grove
The kiss turning feral and darkening
Innocent gazelle eyes
To the very open eye of death's girl.

Each tree's foliage has its dialect, and if you've passed wind-school's first grades and mastered *sough, whisper, zephyr* you'll find, in a time of similar receptivities, the analog of a Philodemos or Meleagros, a Longus or Lucianus. Let no one say that nature now no longer speaks to technocratic youth; technocratic youth no longer speaks to nature. Therefore the immaterial and disconnected means of mass communication where, by some expressive phonologic pox, a Swede proposes *x* in Russian and is commanded something else in English from Japan.

Poor Alexander, barely named Great, you went to bathe in a minor river's frigid waters and orphaned the world of its major tongue. Unimaginable! In other words, inconceivable for anyone not called Martin Heidegger. But thankfully, next to the unimaginable is also the fantastic, which is more intelligible to us the harder it is to gloss it from any of the senses to the rest.

In the realm of aural imagination and in terms of simple echolalia alone, it takes more than "wind on leaf" to recall texts. But "nightingale up from water flow" egresses into image. The tumbling, murmuring, the diminuendo, become, with each hearing, games of multiple dimension which, to any but a first-class ignoramus of the senses, lilt in a myriad ways and startlingly enrich our visual plane. We stand in awe of Rothko, Klee, never asking how they reached autocatharsis. The eye accepts deceit; shrewdness never. Profit has no grace, and the painter knows.

Light rain falls downhill on the elms and soon January bikes by, whistling. The two small ships are one. Paradise won by lottery is impossible. Farewell omnipresent Jeremiahs! Spring's smudge is always rosy-fingered.

Steps à la Tchaikovsky

It is already an achievement to analyze a stirring, or fix it in tenths of a second without reality showing the slightest rift. But giving matter a free hand to lose what gravity it must to try and fly with you is grace.

Nowhere does God return repentant, except where you were happy but didn't say. The innocent reveals whole light. And nature pays.

Small closed rotating pomegranates
since trees are also ignorant of dusk
in Judapan's upper gardens
but light traverses one by one
easily woken signs of leap and spread
all scales
clock-like children of the trees
basso continuo of silk blue-mauve
why chase left's destiny with a right foot?
from Odessa's unconfirmed waters
here sprouted pansy there mauve church
to Odyssey's transparencies
everywhere the eggs of little griefs
lanterns of supine nights extinguished and not
and nowhere love
before the Russians and the Greeks
love nowhere
con brio the command
sonic mares thrill water's heartbeats
as if suddenly you see alight
on Svolen's hills that lit
in the dark
old red of most ambushing day
small closed rotating pomegranates.

Where does this uphill torrent lead? The moment's pause, as if eternal? The people of the ancient speech exist, as also abandoned bowers. Ace pomegranate, marvelous alpha! Time is squeezed tight and forced to trade: girls! high heels! small squares of glass! Every one hundred turns of grief, we must produce a joy. Justice.

PAS DE DEUX

The li li lilt   Ly ly lyric of a slight
lo the upper hand   graze of elbow
Two three five nine   Blow it down or blow it up   two five eight
black you're white   little string or little cat   sixteen thank you
                                  Make me king
                                  dress of wind

Friendship between two senses is often the start of an erotic tale. Touching, you see, and what the mind devises descends from other floors. O children of metal and of stone, but also vertigo and rhythm! We live for a handful of good, let time's carelessness beware! It will be punished. If maybe sudden gusts don't ring zero's essential song.

Lumini and Sombri

Sometimes your solitude becomes hard exact stone; others, a simple feather. It's that sometimes you find it forming in great crowds, then in deserted parks where even the ducks ignore you, withdrawing to the grass to sleep. You then feel despair leaving your mouth, without perhaps the force of a poisonous drug but also without, at least, its therapeutic value. You endure a clip from a silent film. And suddenly, the letters you had not yet started to speak begin to shape, in unexpected ways, definite questions. Is despair's core a *deeper hope?* Then isn't solitude the *only value* forcing its revelation?

But wait. Because here, beside the official teleprompter, another one intrudes, less shrewd, playful with words, but also more intelligent, fitting the fleeting truths to the only reality. Surely if certain words look similar it must mean they are family, are kin. In which case, an act by the same faces in the same circumstance acquires, willingly or not, a much more convincing verisimilitude in terms of reality. We need great distance and equal width to face the phenomenon. Which one? The one of life and how to rightly understand all its mysteries.

Circuitous round earth unwinds an alien light.

This is what it's about. It is this light which all those who have slipped the brakes of daily friction – sculptors and painters, philosophers and authors, musicians and poets – seek to transmute and worship as the one true element of this world's second, and real, order.

A myriad microscopic lucid grains (Lumini) and as many dark ones (Sombri) share vision's surface, as George Sarantares used to say. Occurrences occurring to occur in concurrent and discurrent situations intercur until the deeper hope at last is born. We all have our way and, how strange, it is the way our art most often finds its easiest expression. A single pass through Florence's Uffizi makes you perambulate for days under some gold dust, as if Angelico's kin. A similar feeling rises from lines of Hölderlin or Shelley, or some Mozart and Haydn motifs. Just try now to sort through the National Gallery and the Tate, Vivaldi and Mahler, Rimbaud and Eliot, Valéry and Blake.

And yet you do. Indeed you easily deduce a general conclusion. In imagistic arts – especially if you begin in Crete, Thera, and Egypt (just for their colored friezes), through the Etruscans to the pre-Renaissance – the Lumini preponderate by far. In music arts they're even. And in verbal arts, not only do Sombri preponderate but cover ninety percent of international letters. Why? Ancient lyric poetry buzzes and overflows with health, as if you'd squeezed a word-grape, perfumed each moment by its juice. Even in periods of so-called decadence, including the Palatine Anthology's votive epigrams, no sigh is heard, just honor, order. The tragics overturn exactly these, showing their other face.

O dangerette, how small you seem for all your horrors! How great the equalizing force of time that speeds the slow and slows the quick until life's weight, if it's authentic, if it flows from a source, reaches such utter limit that it weighs on us exactly like its absence. One day justice will be called "a precise moment," as exemplified by the great architects and mariners who set the paradigm: Iktinos, Anthemios, Isidoros, Kosmas of Spetses. Justice will be meted out at midnight, as shown by Atlantis, in a deeply blue outdoors fragrant with thyme. Then, whichever moon desires to emerge will be received.

ONE MINUTE'S INTERMISSION

A thin wire of water in the night, so silver it turns to a ribbon on a girl's hair, is constantly surprised by my own thoughts, which I let run beside it while the whole sky empties; low the compassionate, the entrail-bearing moon, and the lambs of the north keep running, bleating toward an endless, endless Thessalon Nike.

Night's natives redden regardless. Just as the moment strikes. A rose was given each of us, and each must tally when and how to help the day arise. Is it by quartering the sun, as some Pythagorians upheld?

Or by replacing alternately the length and width, the height and depth of daily life's dimensions? Reaching the point where they change our globe's own shape?

No life was ever fulfilled as prefigured. Luck is not manufactured, though its organization in some arena is completed in our ignorance. We are the crew of an ocean liner that always travels and always stays in place. Like the cat, turning to bite its tail. An eternally rotating closed circle. Yet a circle, which, as many sins as it encompasses, obtains the force of law if inscribed in a stable square. Because clean speech is surf, and redolent its every deviation. A wind, half-Hellespont on its maternal side and half-Aeolian native, carries me at night and we exterminate the omnipresent horror with a simple geranium stem.

I live in the smallest country, the smallest house, the smallest yard, and the largest flowerpots in the world. Watering them is a national affair. Charming them is mine. Let us not forget that it took three hundred million years to perfect a pansy and make each rosebush a princess. Daily in this fecundity, each bud leans for a kiss yet hides. Which one are you? Come and be known. Known your underage hair, your gold coin, your sideways gray-green eyes, your little rosemary slingshot, your New Year's palms, and the already possible perhaps great-grandmother of your sorrow.

RENEW ABLE ASEAG LESYOU TH

This contracted speech recalls the motion of a truck beneath a tree arcade; shade-light, shade-light, shade, shade-light. I don't know if, over a great length of time, the moment ever arrives for these Lumini and Sombri to be equalized as the colors and numbers of roulette are, according to theoreticians. Fact is, whoever buys sensitivity may lose in this life but will always win in the eternal.

Eternally Past or Way Beyond Winter

Antiquity hungers for fingers and olfaction has no nationality. Smoke existed before Heracleitos made it an example, and we are made awkward by old homes, like dogs facing lost owners. We circle, we smell, we leap in the air to steal crumbs of smell from beloved objects – half-open trunks, broken candy, frog songs from the domesticated swimmers of the yard – as each of them strikes us in set intervals and flares on memory's breastplate. It is they, precisely, who help me keep a different kind of order in my life, like rubies on my watch.

Besides, from a different perspective, if something of the old endures, it is never the object itself; it is the undecaying meaning, as we first knew it, entering our minds. Sure, no one builds chapels nowadays, light boats are made of plastic, dovecots nonexistent. We still have the deserted wind across the whitewashed sill, the sound of a salty rope governing a sail intimate with the winds' cheek, the place once held by the solitary cloisters of the birds.

You must discard today's old to gain the past, the eternally past. You have to always be like buds, way beyond winter.

O summers of black grape and idle bee, straw summers, black and white and so light you barely touch, yet regal like figs and with pleats fixed by sea-stitch; caresses who once were gardenias, navigable verandas open to the unguarded winds, bodies supine or turned halfway, the knee too close to the female cove and the lips half-open dripping half-liquid apricot.

Perhaps a kind of temple should be found one day that valorizes light, giving a green leaf to the beaks of lovers. Something like this would certainly be much more difficult for a contemporary architect, who justifiably does not replicate old mansions, but exalts some glass or light metallic constructs in Tokyo or New York. Yet for this very reason is condemned to small improvements in mass housing. I'm not joking. It is a sentencing whose extent has not yet been revealed.

The twenty-first century is barely here, and already a mediocrity of enormous dimension prepares to peek through its cracks, ready to flood and cover the valleys, hillsides, and crests of all five continents with tentacles of construction, eradicating in its path towns, villages, and pastures, with all their herders and cows. Equalization devours us, endows us with the closed air of a military camp. Just try to conceive the vision of a Kore as motile landscape, or the analog of Platonic Cities in skies of azure luster.

A well-limned euphony breathes, laying a mistral atop the earthen tetragram I open like a huge window upon Euvoia's cove each morning. Fair weather! Almost distilled, half of the globe can be discerned from here. You let go. What wily wind tickles the jasmine's little ears in our ignorance; what stalks and reeds you see, chasing each other in the sudden drizzle, frightened as little birds! Every cicada leap is nothing but a new day here, each player of the evergreen surf a Greek-speaking cricket, leafing through July's book of days. Go on, you bluets, campanels, bee-bells and bittersweets, pepper geraniums, myrrh nymphs, dawn-glories, vesper crocus! A sharper-scented day grows from the old, a thundering command from Zeus's larynx.

Who are we then? What do we seek? What does fate write on our country's palm? No, no. The only writ is WEALTHIEST THE LEAST, inscribed in Greek capitals on prows of ships. Earth and water, that is. In Greek, boulder and sea.

O sweet dawn of humanity! Enduring morning. Where the orange never turns to lead but, even in the dark, gold glows the Mediterranean light. Trees and boulders stay as the finger of wind or surf positions them each time, either thrust forward or becalmed.

Where can the people of this place find roof, if not in their own uniqueness? The uniqueness of Islandism, the uniqueness of Aghion Oros, and, most importantly, of the diachronic character of the Language in which, for thousands of years, objects have not changed owners.

All the oceans' antiphonists will never counterweigh the half-smile of a small private September waiting for new cyclamens to ambush it.

We'll understand the true significance of time when it itself deprives us of the ability to measure it.
But there lies the daily evergreen, exactly.
Come, willow words, bud fountains.

So that the virgins' garden be untouched.

I am difficult; a Thucydides inside-out. I bite death so hard that, by the time he gets his bearings, I've eked out a new extension. I never managed to be graced, though I had many spouses; no, not in church.

Here is a NO *I wear well. It reminds me of the pride and courage of some plants who, on the coldest day of the year, spring a bud. For no other reason but to invade the internal affairs of time, whose photograph we've never seen, although it keeps our own; indeed, of our worst moment, to please its whim.*

Absalom, Absalom, where are you? I want your princely hair, the sapphire belting your tunic. Let the fathers of all governments be eclipsed and life return in us, like Mary's baby.

West of Sorrow

Nearby a small rain with all the yet uncut
fruit-trees the immediate relatives and the children
with lavender florets all turned

West of sorrow

For Efessos

Freely beside me the vineyards are running and unbridled
Remains the sky. Wildfires trade pinecones and one
Donkey bolts uphill
           for a little cloud
St. Heracleitos's day and something's up
That even noses can't diagnose:
Tricks of a shoeless wind snagging the hem
Of Fate's nightgown and leaving
Us in the open air of capricorns
                exposed
Secretly I go with all the loot in my mind
For a life unbowed from the beginning. No candles no
           chandeliers
Only a gold anemone's engagement for a diamond
Feeling its way to where? Asking what? Our moon's half-
           shadow needs
You to console even the graves
Homoethnic or not. The crux is that the scent of earth
Lost even to bloodhounds
With its weeds onions and creeks
Must be restored to its idiom

So what! A word contains you peasant of night's green
Efessos! Forefather sulphur phosphorus your fourteenth
           generation
Inside the orange groves gold words
Sharing the scalpel's chisel
Tents as yet unpitched
                others midair
Lost poles suddenly grinding. Sermons
Rise from the seafloor of the facing coves
Twin scythes for theater or temple
Fresh valley springs and other curly streams
Of thus and so. If ever wisdom

Planned circles of clover and dog grass
Another world might live just as before
           your fingerprint

Letters will exist. People will read and grab
History's tail once more. Just let the vineyards gallop and the sky
           remain
Unbridled as children want it
With roosters and pinecones and blue kites
           flags
On Saint Heracleitos's day
               child's is the kingdom.

At the Corner of Puberty and Bud

Humanity Balthus insists is sui-
Cidal – and willing to hear Mozart not
A soul. The old and vastly useless armies rise
And deploy phalanxes lockstepped in place
Cut laurels all you want
                                             no wreath will form.
Time for the cock to shriek slaughter
Before the knife
For colts to strike metal on the naked stone *en masse*
Who is the one of many and what is that one's lot?

The occupant at Puberty and Bud knows something
It is the bloodhound of our smell May trains
And breasts barely thirteen adorn the future. But
Water wants a sleeve before they make you wear it
Wants you to sail the Hellespont sleepwalking or as Amphion
(Some seek unattainables others a cove of boulders
Apart from those who to great lengths seek speed alone
But who I am also frequents the soft heights
Of pubes and ties the end of extreme hearing with Mozart's
                                             palpitations
And so with something cypressy or mauve the future can
Approach where neither the angelic north nor south
Fare well.) Plaintive streams percussive pebbles
                                             Bring high noon
The crisis hour: either the lung of *minus* or
Young Hermes summer's harbinger ascending
A green and piping reed
Casts two or three dovecotted breaths
And what you regard as heirlooms
Release a sound of susurrating length as when
Two or three eons are compressed in a young boy's year

The occupant at Puberty and Bud was right
The fate of nations sometimes turns just like a private person's
Scored on a different pentagram in lightning
The unripe speaks

And with wild vineyards prior to kisses
The painter limns the upper lip
                      A sculpted sea anemone and masses of cicadas.

For a Ville d'Avray

It is ill-forged if cashable
The coin which
Phonetically within a foreign tongue
Declares a tomorrow if not a bull's sharp snorts
Wide avenues the bicyclists traverse so fleetingly and many
Go to repeat their lesson at a small – and for greedy lips –
Conservatory. Passing fairweather also like the mind
The half-covered knee possesses
Before communing with underclothes and their utter murmur
Flesh becomes more initiate and combs slide
Diagonally across the untouched
Until the final moment sheets. An illusion that fell
Asleep forever for whom self-consciousness is lost

You friends of the smallest chapel have you known
The visitation of birds? They're pink and jonquil-studded under
            their feathers
A readable down and humid apex whose passage draws the current
From the open room. O sweet small murmurs
Sudden cries and then calm sights entrancing
Cherry "ahs" single- and multi-pulsed
Swallowed by wind. As if a shiver still unfelt
Already passed its quiver through the fingers
A thousand times the same though you never counted

A town works like a spinnery whose inhabitants
At the right moment cut the thread
With their teeth
And touch walks on silk and jasmine
Under a white camisole ribbon and as if
From a small summer watering can
Rain the subtlest touches a brief recess
Ten violets long that reigns forever
And counts as key to *hedoné* and turns

To the inviolable condition: dogs want their masters
On their knees and girls want drones for beekeepers
If piety were baptized by another name
If churchbells rang wild pigeons
Then hostages would have been snatched
Free from the clergy of the wind
To halls of tender caresses

This is what John the Younger sought within his square's
· Circle: the entrance – heelspurs hard upon the floor –
Of Ajaxes or Bishops of a secret joy whose singularity
They champion. Boughs of silver grass-dark calm
Breasts of exquisite
In your polis I too have lived

Dizzyingly upon the eighth
Color instincts slide and whirl
Like leaves forbidden yellow
Who loiter in a thin rain till
In curls and saltiness they pour
A secret chlorophyll from sparrow
To lillythroat – this way
Tomorrow's aura breathes
The little prime of primavera has no end.

Toward Troy

A strong magpie wind is blowing and the place fills with gorgeousness
One after the other the hills fall into line but the sea's
Forceful slope leaves an unloomed cloudlet over Myrina's heights
To teach the passerby which fate is scored in gold and which
In bronze. Because these two are not two but one is
About how much and of what kind the other
Unfallen snow the peaks seek and the Centaur
Who has lost the trail looks for a stream
A whole life fills his mind with mind and unstruck lightning bolts
Has the Sirocco elsewhere sown its storms?
Or is wheat's navigable high surf swaying the valleys?

Hungry for island the landlocked Thessales sullen as always.
   That way
They set out toward Troy's parts; and the seahorses' goals
    gave fragrance
One olive gave the next its troth and fired the groves like Easter
A headlong calm and then the rise of waters and again
Stone-sculpted boys still at play in a church corner
Forgetting some urn's solitary spout
       invisible

Infant to the breast raised by the Genovesas. And with a heavy
Red atop an azure collar the warriors advance
In loose white pants
    Years that appear endless
    Even if you were born a day ago
A slave lasts as long as his master's briefness
Yet from one calyx to the other the ambrosia-scented water flows
And from a single light monastic in the skies
Opens a wide dome where the grape can fit its astral clusters.
So they were right the one-time prophets: second
Pelagic myrtle in midair and you Amphitrite's fourth
With diamond teeth go bite!

You can catch snapper by its surname in the air if not
The seafloor by its meager beard
Like boats the houses with their yards and closets list
To the side and an ontogenic
Force slowly dissolves their fragrant imprints
From the ancestral olive press of Age's hardened fingers
I speak the truth Myrina's wind blows down
To the Kratego waters. Colandered disyllabs you either read
Or else out loud they memorize you

                    Kissme   seabe   foreI   loseyou

A key turns both sides either you yourself
Close or to all are opened. With open windows sails

                                                      Toward Troy

In Ioulíta's Blue

Both in a shard of Breseis as in Euripus' shell you'll find
What I mean. It needs August's savage apneas to hunger for mistral
So much they leave salt on the eyebrow and in the sky
A blue whose name among the many can be heard
As pleasant but at core is
                    Ioulíta's blue
As if advancing on the passage of an infant's breath
So that you see so clearly
The mountains opposite approach and
An ancient dove-call rip the surf and vanish

If good is holy from the air again
It is recharged. So from her very children
Beauty multiplies and grows us two or three
Times before sleep
Enacts us on its mirror
Reaping clementines or streams
Of philosophers if not
Also a motile citadel of bees in adolescence. It's so.
Grapes make black sun and whiter skin.
Who else but Death contests us?
Who does injustice for a fee?
One consonance is life
                    wherein a third sound enters
And tells what's really thrown out by the poor
And gathered by the wealthy: feline caresses
Easily plaited willow wreaths with capers
Evolutionary words
                    with short one of their vowels
Cytheran kisses. Things like these
Foothold the ivy and wax the moon
So lovers see in what
                    Ioulíta's blue

The spidersilk of fate is possible
To read.

Ai! I've seen sunsets
And tiers of ancient theaters traversed.
Yet time never lent me beauty
To overcome black's victory nor lengthen love's arena
So smarter and more mellifluous within us sound the lark
From its own altar:
A frowning cloud a simple "don't" lifts featherlike
And then it falls you fill fill fill
Your hunger with its rain.
You are the twin of the untouched
And you don't even know it
But go on in the garden's virgin grounds
Tickling and being tickled by girl cousins.
Tomorrow a passing organist will sprinkle us nightflowers
And we'll remain regardless a little not happy
As often in love
Yet from the mastic of earth's clay a taste
Rises heretical half hate and dream
Half nostalgia.

If we still count as humans who
Live under domes transfixed by emerald tritons
The hour will be a half-a-second after noon
And utter perfection
                    fulfilled in a garden of hyacinths
From whom decay has been eternally removed. Something dusky
Which one drop of lemon clarifies and then
You see from the beginning what I meant in clean
Characters inscribed
                on *Ioulíta's blue.*

The Marble Table

ALL AROUND the four the
Three two one L'UNIQUE LE SOLITAIRE
LE MARIÉ À VIE A SA CIGARETTE on a balcony over
       the Mediterranean
And a cup of meanings as difficult and tasty COME I FICHI
      LA MATTINA
Counts what remains. It cannot be summed up
Though you might draw equators with straight lines
The truth requires bent ones. Less of the mind and
      more of
Earth is our second and third substance.

Glad lights of New Orleans percussive multivoiced
Different from Odessa's after or before
      the Trickster
Set out with his navigable
Flammable lofty clouds in the unburnt sky
The umbral fugitive of sounds is jarred
Even if the equator must obey him
Rose tulips azure smoke exhales
And memory and good combine at the same height
Ah roosters of my wakening
      pigeons of my white summons. Not I
But what I love moves me from Venice Córdoba to Ammohostos
      Cairo Alexandria
      ALL OVER THE WORLD
With verbs of the Hellespont fished at high noon

Everything passes minus the soul's weight. Where and how
Change its location? As softly as the agile cat
Bites on her tender newborn napes
To go from house to house so I
With my sorrow's swaddlings
Seek refuge large or small in the unknown

Self-chased by awful shrieks the slayed the clanging weapons
Invisible to mortals low weeping of a daughter whose desired lot has
        not been drawn
In all tongues the i m p o s s i b l e endures

WEST OF SORROW the knitting of all meanings is
Ceaselessly completed
Without a single person given to decode
One dream-interpreter's scripts
Even in light even in middle earth
        with or without dominion
Over an eyelid of cloud two or three stormy waves

Swiftly the soul is wrinkled as when the west wind rises
SI PIEGA IL TAVOLO DI ARMO DA UNA PARTE. Clouds will arrive
More fleeting than the sorrows
Or possible to cut by glass
        shard of full moon
And dissolve. You feel
Stopped but your path still runs you
And the beat of your heart outstrips the clock. So
You arrive at Avignon and Nice and Cap Ferrat
        Menton Lausanne. What else
Can be subtracted for your sake still leaving time
        untouched
Clock gardener scythe rake sprinkler plows.
I mean the secrets of a multiethnic net arrive
As a steam engine gradually grinds down
        the force until
The marble table
Is seized PLEIN DE MOTS LANCÉS AU HASARD and greater
Accord through the irrelevant achieve the four
        the three two one.

As Endymion

Exactly like the upper life sleep has
Its tender valleys. With little churches grazing
          grass before the air
Chewing until they turn to icons
Erasing each other in a sideways sound. Often
Two or three moons promenade. But soon they fade
Beauty endures the pause as a celestial body
Matter has no age. Change is all it knows.
Take it from start or end. Return flows calmly
Forward and you follow
Feigning indifference but pulling
The rope to a deserted Myrtle cove
Not missing an olive tree
Oh sea
You wake and everything renews!
We were so dandled growing up tossing our genes for jacks!
See what a rise Sirocco Sleep arouses from the placid
          dividing it in two! On one
Side I wake and weep for my delights were taken
And on the other sleep
While Eleutherios departs and Ionia fades
A low hill barely visible
Its tender bellies full of curly greens
Across it it harsh contestments
How guard against contingency
When refugee bees swarm and a grandmother
Among misfortune's fisheries succeeds
To eke from her few gold ornaments kids and grandkids

Get rid of danger and it rolls you down one side ignores you
As you had wanted to ignore it once
Reverse it all now in the sham of your unlined garment
Where soot and gold coins touched

Like slime on the holy
                    Strange
How blindly we live yet hang by it
Fresh dove of basil kiss I gave you on my bed
And in my writings three and four unorthographic winds
To dazzle the pelagi but full
Of mind and knowledge keep each vessel on its course
Events do lurch and in the end
Fall down before the humans
But dark has no lantern in the storm
Where's Miletos where Pergamos
Attaleia and where
                              Constant   tino   tinopolis?
In a thousand sleeps one comes awake
                    but it's forever.

Artemis Artemis grab me the moon's dog
It bites a cypress and unsettles the Eternals
Much deeper sleeps whom History has drenched
Light a match to its alcohol
                                    it's only Poetry
Remains. Poetry. Just and essential and direct
As Adam and Eve imagined it – Just
In the pungent garden and infallible to clocks.

Appendices

Afterword: "Eros, Eros, Eros"

"Agape, Odyssea," replies Ioulíta, lowering her eyes. October evening, 1995. Halandri. We are speaking of poetry, the three of us, gathered to Odysseas' side, close so as not to raise our voices. Often, Ioulíta translates for him, because my Greek fails from emotion, or because she is closer, her chair a little lower, her luminous face by his ear. The summer of writing has gone very well, they tell me. Odysseas writes in the morning, with Ioulíta's help, she writes in the afternoon after swimming, while he sleeps. "We are collaborating really," Odysseas adds, describing their morning process. Ioulíta flees the room, embarrassed. Quiet. She returns to offer me a glass of juice. Mention is made of "people, gossip." I remember Elytis in *Apologia to Emberikos*: "the poet's duty is to expose himself irreparably," but grope for the Greek "expose." Odysseas professes to remember nothing. Ioulíta helps me by way of French. In my retranslation, *irreparably* becomes, clumsily, *unrepeatably* (anepanorthota, anepanalipta). "Irreparably!" Odysseas says. Memory. Laughter. "Well then, let us expose ourselves!" he says. We speak of agape's voice… He cannot see me, but holds my face in his hands. Before I leave, we kiss like Greeks, on both cheeks. I return to the night and the autumn jasmine, a heavy, less subtle scent.

I first saw and heard Odysseas Elytis in a public lecture when I was sixteen. My right eye wanders, I see only through the left. For the first and only time in my forty-six years, both eyes focused and I listened transfixed and transported beyond meaning to what the Sufis call ecstasy: to know and experience at once. For two hours I saw two images speak to the *first and second Greece, what is and what could be, Paradise and Hell one matter differing only in the eye of the beholder*: IT IS BIGAMY TO LOVE AND TO DREAM.

Sappho: Tears unbecome the house of poets.

Elytis: Had I thought I'd become just another mourner for this futile world, I don't believe I'd have ever lifted the pen.

The lucid, the just, the generous, the profligately generous, the philoxenous, the Greek: *Don't be afraid of what is written you to feel.* The days after his death, this line from "The Apocalypse" (*Maria Nefele*) detonated my consciousness. He was the tree of which I was a leaf, and now the "huge sussurating poplar of our thoughts" was gone – how go on? *Don't be afraid...* On my return from work, four days away, his two new books, *West of Sorrow* and *The Garden with the Self-Deceptions*, arrive, inscribed in his determined hand, the envelope aglow with the twelve large, incandescent stamps of a Greek icon: the Apocalypse.

The sunlight blazes as it did after my father's death. My friend and I ride our bicycles to the sea, seared. Last October, sitting with Odysseas and Ioulíta, speaking of the woods and ponds and bay and ocean of Cape Cod where I approximate the outrock jutting that is Greece, Ioulíta says softly, longingly: "You must have bicycles?" She is the Kore of his eye. Their love is immense, modest as the Cycladic effigies, their devotion fills and has filled the air they have allowed me to witness between them for ten years with the pure, imagined and enacted bell of their offering: poetry, love, bigamy, the miracle of *what is and what could be*, embodied.

In 1980 I sent Odysseas a tape of some of his poems I'd brought into English. I began this effort shortly after I arrived in the U.S. in 1967, out of a need to share his lacerating, transcendent force with those I was coming to love, who seemed to long for Elytis's *possible* as if born to it, yet deprived of its knowledge as if by some cruel fiat since birth. In 1977 I sent him my first book. He stunned me by replying. After my second, another note. I gained courage and sent the tape. "You have given my music," he wrote. "I dream of an entire book... *The Monogram* especially." So began this singular honor. We are shy. Years pass between visits, communications. Books cross the Atlantic. Silences fill our visits. Heat drapes its wet mantle over us, those few July afternoons on Skoufa Street, the bed, the desk, the chair, all within reach, while poetry's *possible* defies the walls to the Ionian and the Aegean around us. I always walk back to my mother's house after our visits, two, three, four hours suspended between seas, his light embroidering my soul like his beloved dolphin: "... *I saw the gold flashes and the arcs in light, like the sheerest net cast and raised, cast and raised, in rhythm, one, two, three, four, until the shapes enlarged,*

clarified and leapt from the water scattering a myriad drops, a fringe of
foam around them, then finally their pointed heads diving straight down
at our side, tails broad for a moment in the air, embroidering the blue, a
ceaseless embroidery until the needle and the pelagic tablecloth both
vanished, leaving the soul alone in the victorious procession – weightless,
unwrinkled, the soul free in the light, the sharp interminable brilliance."

He is the homeland of my nativity, the father of my poems. Without him, instantly, Atlantis is swallowed by meeting seas. And then, by mail, the consubstantial song unfolds yet from those lips. My father's last words: "Do not weep – if I return it will be through your joy," and Odysseas' "*Poetry begins where death is robbed of the last word*... the generous human freedom that believes not only the *extant* but also the *possibly extant*, and so passes into a dimension of divine theory where *eros, a simple tree in a storm*, or *a song* are now equivalent," conjoin.

It is less than a week since he left. Soon I will begin my final sojourn through his final songs. I remember weeping the whole length of *The Little Mariner*, bringing it through to my accented English. This is the dream I had the night I finished:

AFTER THE LITTLE MARINER

I woke up in the dark
of a moon steamed against glass
black as if glazed with ebony
or soft lead handled in the blind
of another's dream and he
the crossroader
the atmospheric horseman
the marksman who can calm the deep
by taking a teenager

down from his constellation and instructing
him to walk across the surf then kneel
inside the pelago a broadcast
charging the elements
with Rilke's terror as my soul
rang in the air above

the bedclothes rustled though my limbs
on the bed were paralyzed
transparent

I could see
a ribbon song begin
from the lungs of his penis
inside my body like a swallow
of ice-cold milk in August
gleaming and slow like mercury
upstream and through my lips
and then my soul
fell into or my body rose.

"Look, look: the dead – I do not fear the dead, I do not pity them –
Death shall have no dominion. It 'is in our future.' 'We are all in our
future!' Let's go! Music! Horses! Lights!"

(ODYSSEAS ELYTIS, *The Girls*)

– Olga Broumas

Notes

and where Lord Byron died. The French painter Dela-
croix has a famous painting drawn from this battle,
Greece Expiring on the Ruins of Mesolonghi.

WHAT ONE LOVES: *The Travel Sack*
Otto tis eratai in the original, in Attic Greek.

THE LITTLE MARINER: *Spotlight b*
All scenes are set in Ancient Greece. Miltiades: com-
manding general in the battle of Marathon, 490 BC. Aris-
teides: general of the same time, known as Aristeides the
Just, famed for his logic and lack of personal ambition.
Pheidias: sculptor of the fifth century BC, particularly
known for his work on the Parthenon and the gold and
ivory statues of Athena and Zeus. The Thirty: junta of
tyrants. Phokion: Athenian general and statesman.

ANOINT THE ARISTON: *viii–xiv*

IX   pelago: small sea with islands.

XI   Armstrong: the astronaut.

XII   consubstantial: *homoousios*, term taken from the Greek
       Orthodox credo, applicable to Jesus, who is believe to
       be of one and the same substance as God, his father, in
       opposition to the *homoioousian* belief that the son is
       essentially like the father but not of the same substance.
       One of the major differences between Orthodox and
       Catholic doctrines.

WITH LIGHT AND WITH DEATH: *8–14*

8   In homage to Sappho and the fragmentary nature of most
       of her surviving lyrics. One of several poems in the
       archaic forms.

11   Written in the style deriving from *boustrophedon*, literally
       as the bull turns (in ploughing), in which lines of words
       in capitals and with no breaks between them were in-

scribed, usually on stone stellae, alternately left to right, right to left, left to right. *Boustrophedon* gave way to a left-to-right style that retained, for a time, the lack of spaces between words.

12   The Virgin Mary is much loved in Greece, and her shrines and chapels are distinguished by a plethora of affectionate, geographical, historical, or miracle-evoking appellations.

13   Sikinos: Aegean island.

WHAT ONE LOVES: *Aegeodrome*

Aegeodrome: wordplay off the Greek word for airport, *aerodrome*, whose components are air, *aero*, and runway, *drome*. The catalog is richly and sensuously varied in the original by wide use of dialect and regional speech.

THE LITTLE MARINER: *Spotlight c*

Set in Byzantium.

ANOINT THE ARISTON: *xv–xxi*

XVII   Hegeso, St. Ecaterine: place-names.

XIX   blisses: Greek has a word, *hedone*, root of hedonism in English, that encompasses the specific sensations leading to and culminating in orgasm. The French call it *jouissance*.

XXI   Hermes, leg flexed: it was a significant breakthrough in the history of Greek sculpture to separate the legs, flexing one of them, thus giving the figure fluidity, subtlety, and engagement from any perspective, compared to earlier works that had primarily frontal appeal.

WITH LIGHT AND WITH DEATH: *15–21*

15   Aegina: Aegean island; Mytilene: capital of Lesbos, a large Aegean island, where Elytis's family is from and where he lived, in part, as a child.

17　This poem is written in Ancient Greek in the original. I have tried to retain some of the formality and stately cadence made possible by its intricate syntax. Kore: literally, daughter, young woman; female of a type of early Greek statue, the Kouros, characterized by a frontal approach, arms joined to the sides of the body, legs joined to each other, and a consistent, haunting, very beautiful enigmatic smile.

19　Psara: place-name.

20　This poem does not have a literal coherent meaning in the original. Its appeal is lyrical, emotional, a breakdown of speech in the face of (what I interpret as) a call from the other side.

21　Horn-head: translation of *Keratios*, the proper name from the root *keras*, horn; it suggests both Devil and cuckold, deceiver and deceived.

WHAT ONE LOVES: *The Snapshots*
　　The Snapshots: in Greek, the word for snapshot, *stigmiotypon*, is composed of the words *stigme*, moment, and *typos*, print, or type. The poet puns on this in "I'd wrested types from moments."

a　Place-names here refer to islands, and seaside or riverside cities.

b　Place-names refer to Greek islands.

　　Solomos: Greek poet, author of Greek national anthem.

THE LITTLE MARINER: *Spotlight d*
　　Scenes One through Three are drawn from the successful battle for independence against the Turks in the 1820s. Androutsos, Karaiskakis, and Kolokotronis are heroes of this revolution.

Aerios Pagos is the Greek Supreme Court; it has retained its name from antiquity to the present.

Kapodistrias: first governor of free Greece; the Mavro-michaels led a mutiny against him in 1831, and, after killing him, perished themselves.

Venizelos: early twentieth-century statesman.

Makarios: Archbishop Makarios, National Leader of Cyprus, whom the military junta of 1967 attempted to assassinate; this failed attempt led to their downfall shortly thereafter.

Chronology

"Sun the First," 1943; from *Sun the First*.

"The Hyacinth Symphony," 1939; from *Orientations*.

"Famous Night," 1939; from *Orientations*.

"Ode to Picasso," 1948; uncollected until 1974; in *The Half-Siblings*.

"Beauty and the Illiterate," 1960; from *Six and One Regrets for the Sky*.

"Daughter the North Wind Was Bringing," 1979; from *The Tree of Light and the Fourteenth Beauty*.

"Small Green Sea," 1979; from *The Tree of Light and the Fourteenth Beauty*.

"Villa Natacha," 1973; part one of a three-part poem, first published in *Tram*, with an original sketch by Picasso, a colored lithograph by Laurens, and Matisse decorations from the journal *Verve*.

"The Monogram," 1972; a book-length poem.

"Maria Nefele," 1978; a book-length poem, from which I have given parts in the dialogue format of the book, but out of sequence. *Nefele* is the feminine form of *nefos*, cloud. In its plural form, *Nefelae*, it was the name given to the gods of the new natural order in Aristophanes' play by that name.

Villa Natacha and *The Monogram* were written while the poet was away from Greece, in the difficult years of the military dictatorship (1967–74).

Open Papers published in 1983.

Little Mariner published in 1985.

Outrock Elegies published in 1991.

The Garden with the Self-Deceptions published in 1995.

West of Sorrow published in 1995.

About the Author

Odysseas Elytis was born in Herakleion, Crete, in 1911. His *nom de plume* fuses three important Greek concepts: *eleftheria* (freedom), *elpitha* (hope), and the *Eléni* (Helen of Troy), which are always present in his poetry. His first book was published at the outset of World War II (1940) and was followed by a publishing history that spans more than half a century and includes poetry, essays, and translations into Greek from Rimbaud, Genet, García Lorca, Mayakovsky, Ungaretti, and Brecht. The author of some of the most innovative and influential original poetry of this century, he was awarded the Nobel Prize for Literature in 1979. He died in Greece on the last day of winter in 1996.

About the Translator

Olga Broumas, born in Syros, Greece, has translated three volumes of poetry and a volume of essays by Odysseas Elytis, and has published five volumes of original poetry. She is the recipient of the Yale Younger Poets Award and NEA and Guggenheim fellowships. She is Fannie Hurst Professor at Brandeis University.

COLOPHON

The typeface is Janson Text, created by Hungarian traveling scholar Nicholas Kis in the 1680s. The face, designed while Kis worked in Anton Janson's Amsterdam workshop, inspired revivals by both Merganthaler and Lanston Monotype in the 1930s. Adrian Frutiger and others at Linotype contributed to this 1985 digital version. Design and composition by Valerie Brewster, Scribe Typography.